FEMINISM FROM A to Z

BY
GAYLE E. PITMAN, PHD

Magination Press • American Psychological Association • Washington, DC

Published by
MAGINATION PRESS ®
An Educational Publishing Foundation Book
American Psychological Association
750 First Street NE
Washington, DC 20002

Magination Press is a registered trademark of the American Psychological
Association.

For more information about our books, including a complete catalog, please
write to us, call 1-800-374-2721, or visit our website at
www.apa.org/pubs/magination.

Typeset by Circle Graphics, Columbia, MD
Illustrations by Laura Huliska Beith
Printed by Sheridan Books, Inc., Chelsea, MI

Library of Congress Cataloging-in-Publication Data
Names: Pitman, Gayle E., author.
Title: Feminism from A to Z / by Gayle E. Pitman, PhD.
Description: Washington, D.C. : Magination Press, [2017] | Audience:
   Age: 15+ | Includes bibliographical references and index.
Identifiers: LCCN 2017001268 | ISBN 9781433827211 (pbk.) | ISBN
   1433827212 (pbk.)
Subjects: LCSH: Feminism—Juvenile literature. | Feminists—Juvenile literature. |
   Women—Social conditions—Juvenile literature.
Classification: LCC HQ1154 .P588 2017 | DDC 305.42—dc23
LC record available at https://lccn.loc.gov/2017001268

Manufactured in the United States of America
10 9 8 7 6 5 4 3 2 1

CONTENTS

WHY TEENS NEED FEMINISM

Adolescence is scary. Especially if you're a girl. Once you hit the age of 13, your sunny disposition gets gobbled up by the Surly Attitude Monster. And then, the Hormonal Beast gets in on the action. Now it's all over. You become a partying, drug-using, emotionally unpredictable, and sexually ravenous . . . well, Hormonal Beast with a Surly Attitude.

Right?

Obviously this is an exaggerated stereotype. And in many ways, it's not even true. That's the good news. The teen years can be a bumpy emotional ride, for sure. However, most teen girls have good relationships with their parents, and many are confident and successful academically. Increasingly, teen girls are choosing to delay sexual activity—and when they do become sexually active, they are highly likely to practice safer sex. For many girls, navigating the teen years isn't at all like a horror story.

That's part of the story. Now, let's look at the flip side:

- 81% of 10-year-olds are afraid of being fat.
- 59% of teenagers drink alcohol, and report drinking to avoid problems and relieve stress.
- Nearly half of all new cases of STIs (sexually transmitted infections) each year occur among 15- to 24-year-olds.

- The U.S. has one of the highest teen pregnancy rates in the developed world. Each year, almost 615,000 American women aged 15 to 19 become pregnant.
- 33% of adolescents in the U.S. are victim to sexual, physical, verbal, or emotional dating abuse.
- Teenage girls are three times more likely than boys to experience depression.

That's the bad news. For a teenage girl, the journey through adolescence has its share of hazards—serious ones. Yet, none of these hazards exist in a vacuum. In fact, in my opinion, all of them share one common denominator:

SEXISM.

That's right. Sexism.

Now, it's overly simplistic to boil issues like drug use, sexuality, body image, and depression down to a single factor. However, imagine for just a moment: What would happen if girls grew up in a world without sexism?

Would girls be so afraid of being fat?
Would some of girls' stresses and problems disappear, reducing the need to drink alcohol?
Would the rate of STIs (and teen pregnancy, for that matter) drop?
Would girls be as likely to be victims of abuse?
Would the risk for depression be so high for girls?

See where I'm going with this?

Unfortunately, sexism is alive and well. Girls and women have come a long way over the years, but we still get treated differently from boys and men. And, even though we have more educational and career opportunities than ever before, we still face gaps in pay, employment, and achievement. Moreover, sexism interacts with other forms of oppression, such as racism, homophobia, and class inequities. These intersections create even more complications for girls making their way through the teenage years.

That's where feminism comes to the rescue.

Think of feminism as a diverse set of tools in a very large toolbox. Some tools allow us to zoom in on sexism and see it clearly. Sometimes sexism shows up in really subtle ways that are hard to see. When that happens, we need a new lens—and that's a good thing to have in our toolbox. Some tools can help us in the immediate moment, when sexism gets in our face and rears its ugly head. Some of these tools, used collectively over time, can help us to eliminate sexism and other "isms" in our broader society.

So many girls and women don't have easy access to the tools of feminism. In fact, if we learn about feminism at all, it probably won't be until after we finish high school. And that is a shame. Imagine how different life would be if, at the age of 13 and suddenly faced with casual sexism for the first time, you had a strong grasp of feminist principles and a hefty feminist toolbox at your fingertips?

Let's be more specific. Here are some situations where feminism can be really helpful:

- If you've ever felt "fat."
- If you've ever been pressured to do something you didn't want to do, or that went against your values.
- If you've ever been afraid to speak up.
- If you've ever been bullied—or been a bully.
- If your confidence has ever felt shaky.
- If you've ever felt unwelcome because of who you are.

Feminism can help you navigate all of these scenarios—and then some. That's why I wrote this book. Because I believe that feminism will change your life.

HOW THIS BOOK IS ORGANIZED

Question: What's the simplest book you can give to a
young child?
Answer: An ABC book!
(That was my answer, anyway.)

Now, I know that you are not a young child. Far from it. However,
feminism is a deeply complex topic. There are *hundreds* of feminist theories and perspectives, some of which are not easy to grasp
without a good foundation. And what better foundation exists than
the alphabet? Learning about feminism is like learning to speak a
different language—and when you learn a language, you need to
start with the basics. Plus, taking an alphabetical journey through
feminism allows you to dip your toe into the water to get a feel for
what it's all about.

In my opinion, the most effective way to build your feminist toolbox is to read this book in order, from start to finish. However, each
entry is designed to stand on its own. If you want to skim through the
table of contents and start with the entries that intrigue you the most,
do that! This book is yours, and you are free to use it as you see fit.

So we'll take a walk through the alphabet, starting with A
and going all the way to Z. In each chapter, we'll focus on a specific

word that starts with that letter—a word that has something to do with feminism in some way. Sometimes it'll be a very feminist word, like "intersectionality," "radical," or "supergirl." A few words, like "brain" and "joke," may seem pretty random and quirky—why would those words be in a book about feminism? And quite a few words, like "knitting," "Easy-Bake Oven," and "don't," probably don't sound very feminist at all. Trust me—all of these words will allow us to explore the world of feminism in some way.

As you read this book, you'll notice that each chapter includes a FEMINIST HERSTORY section, as well as a TRY THIS! activity. Part of developing a feminist awareness involves knowing where we came from and understanding how others paved the way for where we are today. That's where the FEMINIST HERSTORY section comes in. Plus, this section gives you the opportunity to read stories that aren't always told in the history books—because all too often, the contributions of women, people of color, and LGBT people are left out.

Developing a feminist awareness also involves some personal reflection and self-examination. The TRY THIS! sections are action-oriented exercises designed to help you think more deeply about where you've encountered sexism in your life, how you've been affected by it, and how to find power within yourself and among others to resist and dismantle sexism. Some of the TRY THIS! exercises involve self-reflection, while others invite you to participate in hands-on activities. I encourage you to take a pause after reading each entry and spend some time on these exercises. They will deepen your personal relationship with feminism, and they will help you identify which tools of feminism work best for you. They'll also help you flex your feminist muscles—because you never know when you might need to use them!

After you finish reading this book, if you want to plunge further into the world of feminism, go for it! The last section of this book offers suggestions and resources for how to take your feminism to the next level.

A IS FOR

VOTES FOR WOMEN

WOMEN UNITE!

ANGER

"Good girls don't get angry."

Have you ever heard that statement before? You probably have. What's said in that statement has a lot of power. What's even more powerful is what's not said—if you're angry, you must be a "bad girl." And who wants that?

But guess what? Anger is one of our primary emotions. Everyone gets angry! Even babies are capable of expressing anger. It's completely normal, and actually healthy.

Yet boys and girls get different messages about what anger means, and whether it's okay to be angry. Our culture, including the media, assigns a gender to feelings. In the film *Inside Out*, for example, "Sadness" is female, whereas "Anger" is male. Interesting, huh? And that's probably no coincidence—our culture supports and encourages girls to feel sad if they need to, while punishing boys if they even come close to crying. Meanwhile, boys can express anger all they want. In fact, our culture teaches boys that anger is the *only* acceptable emotion. But if a girl gets angry? She might get reprimanded. Or she might be labeled as "crazy," "emotional," or "dangerous." Plenty of movie characters, such as Ursula in *The Little Mermaid*, reinforce that message. Sadly, numerous studies support this; in one study, when men expressed anger, they were seen as passionate, sincere, and committed. In fact, expressing anger in the workplace made it more likely for men to get a promotion. The opposite was true for women; when they expressed anger, they were seen as overemotional, out of control, and unprofessional. No wonder so many girls and women swallow their anger.

Obviously, our gender shapes our relationship to anger. So does our racial identity. A common cultural trope is the notion of the "Angry Black Woman." So many African-American female characters are portrayed as too loud, too angry, too dramatic, or too powerful—even Michelle Obama isn't immune. One magazine cover featured a cartoon drawing of her with an Afro and carrying a machine gun. In a commencement speech that she gave at Tuskegee University, the First Lady shared how she obsessed about her public image: "Was I too loud, or too angry, or too emasculating? Or was I too soft, too much of a mom, not enough of a career woman?" All of this worrying tied to a completely normal human emotion.

These responses to angry girls and women send at least two strong messages: (1) that anger is unladylike; and (2) that there really isn't any reason to be angry, is there? Because things like income inequality, violence against girls and women, body hatred and eating disorders, sexual objectification, and gender disparities in education aren't a big deal or anything, are they? Of course they are! When someone says, "Why do you have to be so *angry?*" not only does it invalidate your feeling, it diminishes the seriousness of the issue you're angry about. And these are pretty serious issues.

So what happens when you feel angry, and you're surrounded by messages telling you that anger isn't okay?

Do you try to cover it up with a smile?

Does your anger sneak out when you don't expect it?

Do you hurt people with your anger, either physically or emotionally?

Do you think bad things about yourself?

Or are you able to express your anger in healthy and productive ways, such as talking about it or writing?

I once heard someone say that "anger is a call to action." When girls get the message that anger is bad, they won't use theirs to take appropriate action. But feminism is all about taking action against injustice. Without anger, social movements wouldn't exist. So remember, listen to your anger, and remind yourself that anger is normal. Then see what happens.

FEMINIST HERSTORY: THE ORIGINS OF THE "ANGRY FEMINIST"

Where did the stereotype of the "angry feminist" come from? Even in ancient times, we see countless examples of the frightening power of angry women. The ancient Hindu goddess Kali, for example, has the power to create and nurture, but she also has the power to destroy. In fact, many artistic depictions of Kali show her as a terrifying, multi-limbed figure, adorned by corpses and the bloody arms of her victims. Another example is Mami Wata, an African water-spirit who is a healer, a protector, and a nurturer, whose powers can potentially go out of control and lead to destruction. Like Kali, she is sometimes shown as a loving, motherly figure but in other depictions is entangled with serpents and wears a menacing expression. And then there's Hera, the Greek mother goddess who had a vengeful streak when crossed. There are countless images throughout ancient history of destructive female anger being unleashed—often in the face of injustice.

More recently, the notion of the "angry woman" has been used in deliberate ways to undermine movements towards gender equality. During the women's suffrage movement—often referred to as the "First Wave of feminism"—political cartoons lampooned women's anger in an effort to belittle their efforts towards gaining the vote. Look at this example, and you'll clearly see how the suffragettes' anger was chalked up to them being unmarried, ugly, or just overall man-haters.

This is a postcard created and distributed by a company called Millar & Land. This particular postcard was printed circa 1909, although postcards like these were common in the late 1800s and the early 1900s, when women were trying to secure the right to vote. The message was clear: if you join the suffrage movement, you'll end up being an ugly, angry spinster. *Credit:* © The March of the Women Collection/Mary Evans Picture Library

The same tactic was used again in the 1960s and 1970s, during what became known as the "Second Wave of feminism." Back then, girls couldn't play sports in school, and they couldn't always take classes in subjects that interested them. A woman could be turned down for a job just because she was female. She could also be fired from her job for getting pregnant. She couldn't get her own credit card or get a mortgage in her own name. These were the conditions that gave rise to the Women's Liberation movement. But, instead of taking girls and women seriously, many people made fun of them for being angry. Feminists were so angry, people thought, that they went so far as to burn their bras. (Contrary to popular belief, feminists never took organized action by burning bras.) Or, in some cases, people would intentionally provoke feminists into anger, then blame them for being angry and unreasonable. Phyllis Schlafly, a conservative activist who opposed the Equal Rights Amendment (ERA), famously baited feminist Betty Friedan into saying, "I'd like to burn you at the stake!" The ERA was a proposed constitutional amendment that would grant equal rights to all citizens regardless of gender. It was a controversial piece of legislation, and many people—both men and women—wanted to prevent it from passing. Making women look angry and emotionally unstable was a very effective tactic; the ERA was never signed into law.

Even today, examples of the "angry feminist" (and its cousin, the "angry activist") abound. In 2012, members of the Russian punk rock band Pussy Riot—well-known for its unapologetic and angry protest music—were jailed for their opposition to President Vladimir Putin. Activists involved with the Black Lives Matter movement are routinely called out for being "extremists," motivated by "unchecked anger"—and blamed for tearing apart their communities. And then there's Hillary Clinton, who has been constantly criticized for being dishonest, ugly, distant, too feminist, not feminist enough, poorly dressed, too expensively dressed, and "hawkish" (otherwise known as *angry*). In his book, *The First Family Detail: Secret Service Agents Reveal the Hidden Lives of the Presidents*, author Ronald Kessler says, "When in public, Hillary smiles and acts graciously. As soon as the cameras are gone, her angry personality, nastiness, and imperiousness become evident. . . . Hillary Clinton can make Richard Nixon look like Mahatma Gandhi." Clearly, one man's passion and commitment is another woman's lack of professionalism—a dangerous double standard that perpetuates gender oppression.

TRY THIS!

Sometimes it's hard to know when we're feeling angry, why we're feeling that way, and what to do about it. So we're going to use a technique that can help name for us what's going on. It's called externalizing the problem. The next time you're feeling angry, try this exercise.

You'll need:

- A pen and notebook
- A set of colored pencils
- A sketch pad

Sit for a moment and let yourself feel your feelings. What thoughts are going through your mind? What sensations do you feel in your body? Take a few minutes to write down responses to these questions.

On a scale from 1 to 10 (1 being "not angry at all" and 10 being "the angriest I've ever felt in my life!"), how angry are you feeling?

Now, try to visualize your anger as if it were a character. This is the "externalizing the problem" part. What color is your anger? What shape is it? How does it move? What are its positive and negative characteristics? Draw your anger, and give your anger a name.

Now that you've personified your anger, you can have a conversation with it. There are lots of questions you can ask Anger. Here are some examples:

- What does Anger need right now?
- How well do you know Anger?
- Does Anger try to disguise itself as something else?
- Does Anger hide? What do you think would convince Anger that it's okay to come out?
- Does Anger come out too much, or too aggressively? What can you do to keep Anger under control?
- What is Anger trying to tell you?
- How will you know when Anger's issue is resolved?

Spend some time writing responses to each of these questions. It's amazing how differently we can relate to Anger when we can actually see it!

B IS FOR

MOLECULAR STRUCTURE OF **B**¹²

GOOD FOR THE BRAIN

DISCOVERED BY DOROTHY HODGKIN

BRAIN

Sara, a 6th grader, always did well in school. She loved reading classic literature, and she was a whiz at math. The previous summer, she'd attended science camp and had a blast. School was a place where Sara thrived. Until the teasing started.

"Ugh! You're so smart!"

"Only ugly girls go to science camp!"

"Brain!"

Sara started to feel isolated. School wasn't fun anymore. So what did Sara do? She started censoring herself. She stopped raising her hand when she knew the answer. She dumbed herself down. And soon enough, Sara became part of the popular crowd.

While this isn't every girl's story, far too many middle and high school girls have this experience. So many girls are encouraged to do their best academically and succeed but then are also bombarded with stereotypical counter-messages that discourage them from being "too smart" or "too successful." How do those counter-messages work?

Imagine this: A group of Asian-American women are asked to take a math test. Before they take this test, though, they have to fill out a personal questionnaire. What these participants don't know is that half of them are completing a questionnaire about being female, while the other half are completing a different questionnaire focused on being Asian-American. The big question is, does the focus of the questionnaire have any impact on their performance on the test?

The researchers discovered that participants who were given a questionnaire about being female did far worse on the math test compared to those who filled out a questionnaire about being Asian-American. The "female" questionnaire activated a common stereotype for those participants—the idea that girls and women can't do math. Why did this happen? Researchers call this phenomenon *stereotype threat*, which involves inadvertently conforming to a negative stereotype about one's group. Research has shown that stereotype threat can affect academic performance, game-playing skill, scores on standardized tests like the SATs, and athletic performance, among other things. It's an insidious process, and it can have significant effects on a person's self-esteem.

There is a flip side, though. Instead of stereotype threat, sometimes people experience what's called *stereotype boost*. This happens when a positive stereotype is activated for someone, ultimately leading to improved performance. The participants who completed the questionnaire about being Asian-American experienced this effect. For them, the stereotype that "Asians are good at math" was probably highlighted—and that, in turn, led to a boost in their math test score.

One more factor might be at play. How others perceive us can also have an effect on our performance and on our perception of our own abilities. In a classic 1968 study, researchers gave elementary school students an IQ test, then shared with teachers the names of 20% of the students who, based on their test scores, were "intellectual bloomers." What the teachers didn't know is that the "intellectual bloomer" label had nothing to do with their actual test scores; these students were selected randomly, regardless of their score. Eight months later, when the researchers retested the students, they discovered that the students labeled as "intellectual bloomers" scored significantly higher than the rest of the students. The converse was true as well—students who were thought to have poorer test scores did worse overall on the IQ test at the end of the year. This phenomenon is called the *Pygmalion effect*, named after the character in Ovid's *Metamorphoses*. Clearly, how teachers perceive their students' abilities has a major effect on their students' level of success.

When you combine the effects of stereotype threat and the Pygmalion effect, it's easy to see how negative messages can affect things like overall school performance, grades in math and science, interest in attending college, and future career goals. Too often, girls are surrounded by negative messages about being smart; for example, girls who raise their hands in class and share their knowledge might run the risk of being branded as a "know-it-all." At the same time, those same girls might be encouraged in a variety of ways to be attractive and sexy. When those messages are in play, girls may feel like they have to choose between smart and pretty—and if pretty wins, their academic performance is likely to take a hit. Research shows that girls who start dating early might get popularity points, but often their grades suffer as a result. Other studies show that girls who identify as extremely feminine and who place a high value on feminine attractiveness tend to do worse in school.

But here's the deal. Right at this moment, your brain is going through a serious growth spurt. Rapid-fire connections are being made in a part of your brain called the *prefrontal cortex*, which is right at your forehead. Lots of skills are associated with the prefrontal cortex: planning, organizing, decision making, complex problem solving, critical thinking, etc. All of these skills help you do well in school and ultimately succeed in your future career. If you think about it, your brain's development is allowing you to grow more powerful. And yet, too often, the cultural messages that surround us dampen the power of your brain's potential.

So all those messages that are out there, discouraging girls from succeeding? *They're lies.* Your brain's natural instinct is to grow and become stronger. Don't get in its way! Plus, doing well in school makes us feel good about ourselves and our abilities. That's something everyone wants.

FEMINIST HERSTORY: WHOM CAN YOU THANK FOR YOUR CELL PHONE?

Have you ever wondered how your Wi-Fi connection works? Or how you can (usually) send an e-mail through a secure connection? In order to explain this, you'll need a crash course in communications physics. Don't worry—we'll keep it simple! And yes, there is a point to this. Just hang in there.

When you listen to the radio, you're using a conventional wireless signal. That signal has a frequency, usually specified in megahertz (MHz) or gigahertz (GHz). For example, when you listen to 100.3 on an FM stereo receiver, that means that the signal is at 100.3 MHz. That signal stays there; it doesn't go up to 101.3 or down to 99.3, unless you change radio stations. Easy so far, right?

But there are a few problems with conventional wireless communication. First, you can get interference with a constant wireless signal. You've probably experienced this in a car—if you're listening to the radio, especially if you're getting out of range, you might hear two radio stations at once, with some white noise thrown in there. It's also possible to create deliberate interference with a constant radio signal, and people sometimes do this in wartime situations. Second, it's easy to intercept a signal that's constant, so it's not a great technology to use when you want communication to be confidential.

That's where Spread Spectrum Technology (SST) comes in. It's a form of wireless communication in which the frequency of the transmitted signal varies. The most common way of varying the signal is to use a technique called frequency hopping. With this technique, the transmitter frequency changes multiple times per second, which makes it much harder for someone to hack into your e-mail or wireless connection.

OK. Pop quiz. Who invented this technology? Whom can you thank for your cell phone? (Hint: It wasn't Steve Jobs. Or anyone at Apple, or Google, or any of the big tech companies.)

This is a publicity photo of Hedy Lamarr taken in 1940, shortly after the release of her first American film, *Comrade X*. According to Lamarr's biographer, after her face appeared on the screen, "Everyone gasped. Lamarr's beauty literally took one's breath away."

The woman in the picture above is Hedy Lamarr. If you don't know who she is, you probably know some older adults who do. Lamarr was a 1940s Hollywood actress during MGM's "Golden Age." She was often called "The Most Beautiful Girl in the World," starring in films with Spencer Tracy, Clark Gable, Judy Garland, and James Stewart, among others. However, even people who are familiar with Lamarr's film career don't know that she was also a scientist and an inventor.

Originally named Hedwig Eva Maria Kiesler, Hedy Lamarr was born and raised in Vienna, Austria. Her first husband, millionaire Fritz Mandl, was a Nazi sympathizer who sold weapons to Adolf Hitler. During their four-year marriage, Mandl treated Lamarr as his "trophy wife," taking her to business engagements and high-profile social gatherings. At these meetings, Lamarr paid attention and absorbed a lot of information about advanced weaponry. Later, she left her husband and fled to London, where she met Louis B. Mayer. They came to the United States where she received a new name and signed her first movie contract. Shortly afterwards, she met American composer George Antheil, and at that point she was able to use the knowledge she'd gathered about weaponry to help the war effort. Together, she and Antheil developed the idea of changing radio frequencies rapidly to prevent enemies from detecting messages. This "Secret Communications System" was patented when Lamarr was 26 years old.

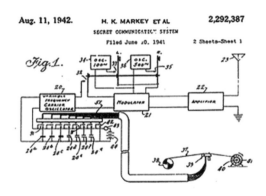

Lamarr's "Secret Communication System" was patented on August 11, 1942, at the height of her film career. It is the technology we use today to support Wi-Fi, cell phones, and other forms of wireless communication.

Ultimately, their invention wasn't used during World War II because the technology in the 1940s wasn't developed enough to make it work. However, twenty years later, their "Secret Communication System" was implemented during the 1962 Cuban Missile Crisis.

Hedy Lamarr didn't earn any money from her invention, and it took over 50 years for her to receive any recognition. In 1997, Lamarr and Antheil won the Electronic Frontier Foundation (EFF) Pioneer Award. Later that year, Lamarr was given the BULBIE Gnass Spirit of Achievement Bronze Award—which, in the science and innovation fields, is like receiving the Lifetime Achievement Award at the Oscars. She was the first woman ever to receive this award.

Who knew that such a glamorous movie star would have invented such important technology? And yet, here's one of Lamarr's most famous quotes:

"Any girl can be glamorous. All you have to do is stand still and look stupid."

TRY THIS!

Let's go on a scavenger hunt! This is a great activity to do with a group of people from your science class, but you can do it on your own too. (It's just more work to do it by yourself.)

If you're doing this in a group, set up a time to meet and ask everyone to bring their science textbook. Set aside about an hour and a half for this activity.

Give each person one chapter from the textbook to focus on. If you have a large group, you can assign chapters to partners or small groups. Then tell everyone to read through the chapter, and identify each female scientist that's mentioned. Write down their names and include a brief description of their scientific contributions.

Once everyone is done, count up the total number of female scientists that were identified. Were there a lot, or not very many? Did the results surprise you?

If there's time, go online and search "female scientists." At the top of the Google results page, you'll see the names and images of a number of female scientists. Were all of these individuals included in your book? If there are some that are unfamiliar, click on their names and read about them. Do you think their contributions should have been included in your high school science curriculum?

If a group from your class does this activity, consider sharing your results with your teacher. See if your teacher might be willing to include more information about female scientists in their curriculum.

C C C IS FOR

(NON)CONFORMITY

Have you ever experienced peer pressure? If so, you probably know first-hand how stressful it is. You might be at a party where all your friends are drinking alcohol or smoking marijuana, and they try to get you to do it too. Or, you might be in a relationship with someone who's pressuring you to have sex even though you're not ready. In those circumstances, standing up for yourself can be really scary because you run the risk of losing your friends. For some teens, giving in to peer pressure and conforming to what everyone else is doing feels like playing it safe.

But guess what?

Playing it safe is not safe. And here's an example that shows you why.

Several years ago, I attended a local performance of *The Vagina Monologues*, which is part of a movement intended to raise awareness and stop violence against women and girls. (When you get to the "Violence" chapter, you'll learn a lot more about this movement.) My favorite monologue was the last one, titled "ONE BILLION RISING" (deliberately printed in all caps). The woman who performed that monologue gave an impassioned speech about the importance of taking action. Then she said:

"Raise your fist in the air!"

Almost no one did. Then she said it again, her voice louder, reverberating off the walls:

"RAISE YOUR FIST IN THE AIR!"

I raised my fist. Then she screamed, as loud as she could:

"RAISE YOUR FIST IN THE AIR!!!"

I looked around, my fist still held high above my head. Among the several hundred people in the audience, only a handful had raised their fists. *Why?* I wondered.

Maybe the audience was confused. Is she saying "raise your fist in the air" as a metaphor, or does she *really* want us to raise our fists? It's not typical to be at a theater performance and be asked to raise your fist in the air—in fact, it's kind of a norm violation. But frankly, it's pretty low-risk; by breaking the norm of sitting with your hands in your lap, you're certainly not hurting anyone. And anyway, if the audience really wasn't sure how to respond, you'd think that yelling at the top of her lungs so the walls shook would have cleared up any remaining confusion.

So why, then, didn't people confidently raise their fists?

There's safety in staying quiet—or so we think. In this situation, sitting quietly in a dark theater and enjoying the performance was easy. Merely watching *The Vagina Monologues* is playing it safe. Speaking out against violence, taking action, being willing to be the lone voice in a crowd—that's much harder. Often, we'd rather be accepted by the majority than stand up for what we believe in.

Picture this: You're a participant in a research study, and you're seated in a room with seven other people. You are each given a card that looks like the one on the next page. You are then asked to look at the test line (Exhibit 1) and identify which of the three comparison lines is the same length. *This is easy*, you think. **Obviously it's Line A.**

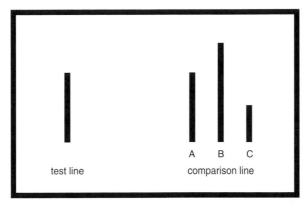

This image is similar to what was shown to participants in Solomon Asch's conformity studies.

"Line B," says the first participant, with confidence in her voice. *What?* you think. *She must not be able to see straight.*

"Line B," says the second participant, with equal conviction. *Hmm.*

"Line B," says the third participant. And the fourth, fifth, sixth, and seventh.

Now it's your turn. What do you say? Are you worried about sticking out like a sore thumb if you give a different answer? Are you starting to doubt yourself? *Maybe I'm the one who can't see straight*, you might think.

And then you hear yourself saying, "Line B." You decided to play it safe.

The seven other participants, as you've probably figured out, weren't real participants. They were confederates in a classic study conducted by Solomon Asch, a social psychologist at Swarthmore University. Asch had coached these individuals in advance to deliberately give the wrong answer. Among the "real" participants—the ones who were in Seat #8—75% conformed to the group and gave the wrong answer at least once during the many trials that were administered.

Almost one-third (32%) conformed *every single time*. They wanted to fit in and be accepted, and they were willing to give the wrong answer in order for that to happen. They, too, played it safe.

If you think about it, conformity is a powerful social tool. If social norms are going to be created and maintained, then you need some kind of social policing system that maintains law and order. Conformity is part of the arsenal of weapons that prevents (and punishes) any norm violations that might occur. In our collective groupthink, nonconformity is analogous to disruption and danger and the conformity police help to keep us safe.

So, back to why "playing it safe" is not safe. It reinforces oppressive, marginalizing, dehumanizing social norms. When we stay silent or fail to take action on things like gender discrimination, unrealistic beauty norms, or sexual violence, we're essentially saying that the status quo is just fine with us. If, on the other hand, we want to end oppressive attitudes, behaviors, and institutional practices, we have to speak out and take action. And that, by definition, involves challenging and violating social norms. Conformity is the enemy of confidence.

FEMINIST HERSTORY: THE MURDER OF KITTY GENOVESE

One early morning in 1964, at about 3:15 a.m., a young woman named Kitty Genovese got home from her shift working as a bar manager. She parked her car and started walking towards her apartment building. A man approached her. Frightened, she started to run away, but he caught her, stabbing her twice in the back.

"Oh my God!" she yelled. "He stabbed me. Help me!" An onlooker yelled, "Let that girl alone!" The attacker ran away.

And then he came back. The attacker found the young woman lying in a hallway at the back of her building. He stabbed her several more times, raped her, and stole $49 before leaving her to die. The entire scene, from start to finish, spanned about 30 minutes. And during that time, no one came to her aid—even though numerous people heard or observed parts of the attack. While some of the facts are in dispute, the case brought the phrase "bystander apathy" into our cultural conversation and raised questions about what causes it to occur.

A few years after this tragic incident, two researchers at Columbia University, John Darley and Bibb Latané, conducted a series of studies to try to better understand this phenomenon, two of which can help us understand why it's so hard to stand up against injustice.

In one study, often referred to as the "smoke-filled room" experiment, the researchers randomly assigned their participants to one of three conditions: either (A) the person was in a classroom alone, (B) with two other participants, or (C) with two "confederates." Within several minutes of the study, smoke began to fill the room; Darley and Latané wanted to see how likely the participants were to report it. While 75% of the participants in group A reported the smoke, only 38% in group B and 10% (!) in group C made any report.

In a second study, better known as the "seizure" study, participants were told that they would be engaging in a communication task via intercom with an individual in a separate classroom. Like in the "smoke-filled room" study, participants were randomly assigned to one of three conditions: either (A) the participant was in a classroom alone, (B) with one other person, or (C) with five other people. During the communication task, the person they're talking to in the other room starts having a seizure. Darley and Latané wanted to see how many people would respond. As it turns out, 85% of those in group A left the room to provide help. However, when other people were present in the room, helping behavior decreased substantially: 62% in group B and 31% in group C left the room to help the victim. Different study, but essentially the same findings as the "smoke-filled room" experiment—the more people that are around, the less likely people are to spring to action.

And why is that? *Diffusion of responsibility.* People are less likely to take action when there are other people around because they assume that others will. *I didn't do anything because I thought someone else would step up.* Unfortunately, when everyone thinks that someone else will take action, the end result is that *no one* takes action.

TRY THIS!

There are many ways to engage in social action. Read the following list of actions. Can you identify ten actions in this list that you'd be willing to participate in, and that feel comfortable to you? Why did you choose them?

Now identify ten actions that you *wouldn't* be willing to participate in. Why did you choose them? Take a few minutes to write about the reasons why you wouldn't engage in these actions.

Choose one activity from the list and do it!

Actions Teens Can Take
- Give a speech.
- Sign a petition.
- Start a petition.
- Write a letter to a newspaper, magazine, or organization.
- Sign a letter that was written by someone else.
- Do an interview for the newspaper, radio, television, or Internet.
- Write an Internet blog post.
- Post about an issue on social media (e.g., Facebook, Instagram, Twitter).
- Distribute leaflets and pamphlets.
- Create leaflets and pamphlets.
- Create political protest art.
- Picket.
- Display a flag or banner (e.g., Pride flag).
- Wear a symbol.

- Participate in a vigil.
- Perform in a political skit, play, or musical event.
- Sing a protest song.
- Participate in a political march.
- Participate in a group protest.
- Participate in a teach-in.
- Participate in a walk-out.
- Engage in silent protest.
- Boycott a product, event, business, or institution.
- Encourage others to boycott a product, event, business, or institution.
- Engage in social disobedience.
- Participate in a student strike.
- Participate in a sit-in.
- Participate in a political fast.
- Participate in a hunger strike.
- Participate in a nonviolent occupation.
- Start a hashtag on Twitter.
- Participate in a riot.
- Engage in video blogging.
- Join a political organization.
- Start a political organization.
- Engage in peer education.
- Speak at a school assembly.
- Speak at a community forum.
- Write a letter to your legislator.
- Meet with a legislator to address an issue.
- Conduct a survey and share the results.
- Raise money.
- Take on a leadership role in your school.
- Take on a leadership role in your community.
- Take on a leadership role at the state or national level.

IS FOR

REFRAMING

DØN'T

My mother saved everything, including books. She's given me old children's books from the 1940s and 1950s, including her entire collection of Nancy Drew books. My grandmother and great-grandmother also had lots of books, and I have some of those in my collection. One of my favorites is titled *Don'ts for Girls: A Manual of Mistakes*. It was written in 1902 by a woman named Minna Thomas Antrim. It's a short book made up of a series of statements, all starting with the word "don't."

Some of the "don'ts" are inspiring, and pretty forward-thinking for the early 1900s:

> *Don't let others do your thinking.*
> *Don't lose faith in yourself if you wish others to believe in you.*
> *Be original. Don't be a poor copy of someone else.*

Some "don'ts" are pretty comical, such as these:

> *You may like to call yourself a "bachelor girl." Very well!*
>   *Don't fail to be a self-respecting bachelor.*
> *Don't be assured of your beauty when men stare. Some men*
>   *stare at any skirted object.*

DON'T go anywhere
with a young
man alone.
Convention
admits no ex-
ception of this
rule

DON'T listen to anything revolting.
There are things in life
that should never
be made known
to a sensitive
girl

10¢

DON'T become mas-
culine if you are
a college girl.
Fit yourself for
a vocation if you
choose, but hold
fast to your girl-
ish personality

DON'T abuse your strength. Young
muscles are delicate. "On the go"
all the time, presages
"off the go"
in later life

18

A few more of the "don'ts" included in *Don'ts for Girls: A
Manual of Mistakes*. Do you think these attitudes are still
present today?

But many of the "don'ts" are downright sexist:

Don't be too positive. A girl who is too assertive is never popular.
Don't oppose or ridicule the opinions of your brothers. Boys
  and men grow crusty when things go crosswise.
God made you for skirts. Don't dress like a man. Girls who do
  are as absurd as boys who are girlish.

What drew me to this book was the use of the word "don't." Compared to boys, girls get bombarded by that word, particularly when it comes to taking risks, trying new things, or engaging in non-feminine behavior. *Don't get dirty. Don't get hurt. Don't walk home by yourself. Don't be late.*

And the word "don't" is sneaky. Sometimes it doesn't even have to be verbalized. When a girl is wearing a white dress, for example, the unspoken message is *don't get dirty.* If she's wearing heels or dress shoes, the unspoken message might be *don't run*—because who can run in heels? If she's sitting in class and thinks she knows the answer, but isn't quite sure, she might think *don't raise your hand.* Even though these aren't obvious messages, this subtle way of reinforcing gender expectations is incredibly effective and quite damaging. Let's talk about why.

Researchers Eden King and Kristen Jones delved into the topic of bias and discrimination by doing a type of study called a *meta-analysis.* This involves combining studies that all focus on the same topic and evaluating the overall results. In their case, they found 90 separate studies that distinguished between subtle and obvious discrimination, and then looked at the relationship between those forms of discrimination and a range of outcomes, including stress, job performance and satisfaction, and physical and mental health symptoms.

Not surprisingly, their analysis found that *all* forms of discrimination were associated with negative outcomes. But here's what's *really* interesting. According to Dr. King's and Dr. Jones' meta-analysis, subtle discrimination is as bad as, and sometimes *worse* than, obvious discrimination. In essence, while it's harmful to tell a girl she shouldn't play outside and get dirty, it's even more harmful to send that message implicitly by clothing her in a fancy dress and shoes and expecting her to stay neat and clean. Here's another example: clearly, it's inappropriate for a teacher to say to a female student, "Girls shouldn't pursue careers in science." That's obviously a biased (and completely inaccurate) statement, which is likely to have a negative impact on that student. But picture this: What if that student was in that teacher's class, and the teacher never called on her? Or, what if the teacher did call on her, but she didn't receive positive feedback in the same way male students did? The messages that are largely invisible are the ones that tend to cause the most harm.

Whether these "don'ts" are obvious or subtle, they all have a not-so-great impact. But every "don't" can be flipped into a "do." Let's go back to *Don'ts for Girls: A Manual for Mistakes*, and I'll show you what I mean.

Here's a "don't" statement:

Don't let others do your thinking.

Now, here's that same statement, flipped into a "do:"

Do your own thinking.

See how much more empowering the second statement feels, compared to the first? That happens for two reasons. First, there's a *framing effect*, which means that the way that information is presented can strongly influence how people react to it. Second, saying "don't," compared to the word "do," tends to evoke a negative response, and we're much more likely to remember negative things than positive things. This is called the *negativity bias.* The combined influence of these two effects makes *don't* a very strong and mighty word.

Here's where a simple series of actions can make all the difference. We can reframe negative statements into positive ones. We can also challenge negative statements that are inaccurate, and then restructure them into positive and accurate statements. If we re-wrote *Don'ts for Girls: A Manual for Mistakes,* here's what that might look like:

> *Do think for yourself.*
> *Do have faith in yourself.*
> *Do be original.*
> *If you wish to be a bachelor, be a self-respecting bachelor.*
> *Do be assured of your beauty.*
> *Do be positive and assertive.*
> *Do challenge the opinions of others.*
> *Do dress in a way that makes you feel good about yourself.*

Imagine if those were the messages girls received in 1902!

FEMINIST HERSTORY: THE STORY OF ADAM, EVE, AND LILITH

> *The LORD God took the man and put him in the Garden of Eden to till it and keep it. And the LORD God commanded the man, "You may freely eat of every tree of the garden; but of the tree of the knowledge of good and evil you shall not eat, for in the day that you eat of it you shall die." (Genesis 2:15–17)*

Most people are familiar with the story of Adam and Eve in the Garden of Eden. ("Don't eat from the Tree of Knowledge" is probably one of the most well-known "don'ts" in history.) Because Eve was created out of Adam's rib, she wasn't his equal; by definition, God's intention was to make Eve subservient to Adam. God made it clear to Adam that there was plenty of fruit in the Garden of Eden, but under no circumstances should they eat the fruit from the Tree of Knowledge.

This is when the serpent comes into the story. Eve knows that she shouldn't eat from the Tree of Knowledge or else she will die, but the serpent says this to her: "You will not die; for God knows that when you eat of it your eyes will be opened, and you will be like God, knowing good and evil." Eve, tempted by the idea of becoming wise, disobeyed God's orders and ate the fruit, then gave some to Adam. And that, as you probably know, ruined it for everyone; as punishment, all women from that point forward would experience pain in childbirth, and their husbands would rule over them. Essentially, patriarchal rule is all Eve's fault, because she couldn't abide by the one "don't" that God issued.

For centuries, religious and non-religious scholars have challenged and reinterpreted the story of Adam and Eve. There's certainly plenty of material for feminists to take apart, particularly the "woman-as-temptress" concept. That motif pops up everywhere in our culture, from school dress codes (girls shouldn't wear spaghetti straps, because that could be a "distraction" to the boys) to rape cases (the way she acted, she must have wanted it!). If you think about it, those contemporary examples trace all the way back to that story in the book of Genesis.

Now, here's a fun fact: Did you know that some people believe that Eve was Adam's *second* wife? According to Jewish folklore, the first woman created was named Lilith. In contrast to Eve, Lilith wasn't created out of Adam's rib—both she and Adam came from the earth. Because of that, Lilith saw herself as Adam's equal, although she quickly realized that Adam didn't feel the same way. When Adam wanted to have sex with her, he commanded her to assume the missionary position and lie below him—and Lilith refused to obey. According to one version of the folktale, Adam said this to Lilith: "I will not lie beneath you, but only on top. For you are fit only to be in the bottom position, while I am to be in the superior one." Lilith continued to protest, so God cast her out of the Garden of Eden and made her into a demon figure. Each version of the Lilith story describes her demonic qualities differently, such as taking on demon lovers and populating the earth with baby demons, capturing babies and eating them, and leading young girls astray.

Then Adam was given a second wife, Eve, who was created from his rib to ensure her obedience to him. Essentially, Eve was God's do-over. (And you can see how well that worked out.)

The Lilith story hasn't carried over into the Christian belief system. However, it is a well-known story in the Jewish tradition. Many Jewish feminists see Lilith as a symbol of independence, strength, and equality.

TRY THIS!

Sexist messages aren't always obvious. In fact, often they're subtle and sneaky. And some of the most powerful sexist messages come from inanimate objects, like clothing.

For this activity, you'll need the following materials:

- Access to a copy machine, or a scanner and printer (if you don't have any of these, that's okay!)
- A pen
- Two different-colored highlighter markers

Let's delve into this further. Make a copy of this chart. If you don't have access to a copy machine or a scanner and printer, you can create your own chart by hand.

	QUALITIES OF ITEM (NOTES)	PHYSICAL PLAY	IMAGINATIVE PLAY	OUTDOOR PLAY (SUNNY WEATHER)	OUTDOOR PLAY (RAINY OR SNOWY WEATHER)	ART ACTIVITIES	FINE MOTOR ACTIVITIES
Girls' clothing							
Boys' clothing							

Go to a children's clothing store and bring this chart with you. Start with the girls' section of the store. Look at pants, shorts, skirts, tops, sweaters, sweatshirts, jackets, coats, socks, and shoes. Record each item under the heading "Girls' clothing." Next to this list is a column labeled "Qualities of item," with some space underneath to take notes. Here are some things to consider while taking notes:

- What colors are featured most often?
- If the item gets dirty, will the dirt show easily?
- How durable are the fabrics and materials?
- How washable are the fabrics and materials?
- How well would items hold up in rain, snow, or other inclement weather?

Now, do this again, this time with items from the boys' section of the store.

Are there items that our culture would deem appropriate for both boys and girls? If so, mark those items with an asterisk (*).

Go back and review your lists. How appropriate is each item of clothing for engaging in physical play, imaginative play, outdoor play in good weather, outdoor play in rainy or snowy weather, art activities, or fine motor activities? Mark each box with either "DO" or "DON'T." What did you discover as a result of this exercise?

E IS FOR

EASY-BAKE OVEN

When I was a child, I wanted an Easy-Bake Oven so badly. But I never got one. "What do you need that for?" my mother said to me. "We have a real oven."

My mother didn't get it at all. You could bake tiny cakes in it! How cool is that? And it was PINK! Our real oven was most certainly not pink.

The Easy-Bake Oven is one of the most iconic toys in history—at least, for girls. It is the prototypical example of a gender-typed toy, clearly and specifically intended for girls. Probably no other toy in history has been so coveted by little girls, and yet so maligned by feminists. Toys like the Easy-Bake Oven are designed to prepare girls for a life of domesticity. On the other hand, toys for boys, such as Erector sets and Legos, tend to prepare them for the paid workforce, emphasizing things like building, problem solving, and physical activity.

Whether we realize it or not, we tend to label everything as "for girls" or "for boys." Case in point: when a woman is pregnant, one of the biggest questions on everyone's mind is whether it's a girl or a boy. Some people go so far as to host "gender reveal" parties after they find out their baby's sex. Why is this information such a big deal? Because once we know the sex of the child, we can start thinking about what to name it, what clothes to buy for it, how to decorate the nursery, and so on. We're relying on a *gender schema*, an organized set of gender-related beliefs, to guide these decisions. If it's a girl, we can name her Olivia, Violet, or Emma, and we can decorate her nursery in pink and gray with elephants. If it's a boy, we can name him Aaron, Caleb, or William, and we can decorate his nursery in a red-and-blue race-car motif. From the beginning, children are exposed to what our culture associates with being a girl vs. being a boy, and those lessons become more internalized over time.

The process of creating a gender schema isn't limited to toys. In our culture, we assign a gender to practically *everything*. We gender clothing, hairstyles, colors, occupations, household chores, movies (ever hear the term "chick flick"?), emotions (remember Sadness and Anger in *Inside Out*?)—the list goes on and on. Sandra Bem, a psychologist who developed and studied *gender schema theory* back in the 1970s, discovered through her research that these gender schemas aren't totally harmless. What they do, in fact, is reinforce gender stereotypes, and then encourage boys and girls to conform to gender-stereotyped behaviors.

Bem's theory doesn't explain everything, though. For example, in our culture, girls seem to have more latitude than boys when it comes to crossing gender boundaries. A girl can build with Legos or play with Matchbox cars, and it's unlikely that she'll get reprimanded for it. A boy, on the other hand, will probably experience consequences for playing with toys meant for girls—and as a result, he'll be less likely to play with them in the future. In fact, if a toy is considered to be feminine, not only will a boy not play with it, he'll probably develop an "EWWW!" response, as if the toy had cooties because it's for girls. They develop an aversion to anything girly and feminine, and Bem's gender schema theory doesn't really explain why.

Later in her career, Sandra Bem wrote a book called *The Lenses of Gender*, which brings her original gender schema theory to the next level. Here's how this new theory goes: We label pretty much everything as "for boys" and "for girls"—that's the first step. But there are other assumptions that we hold subconsciously which drive this process. Children learn to be *androcentric*, which involves valuing masculinity, or boy-ness, and devaluing femininity, or girl-ness. They learn to be gender-polarized, which means seeing boys and girls as polar opposites. If you combine androcentrism and gender polarization, you can see that while boy behaviors may not be OK for girls, girl behaviors are *really* not OK for boys. And lastly, they learn to believe in biological essentialism—that differences between boys and girls are natural and biologically hard-wired. According to Bem, these assumptions not only reinforce gender schemas, they also contribute to sexism and gender oppression in a powerful way.

So, the logical response is to challenge those assumptions and give children non-stereotypical toys to play with, right? Numerous studies show that children who play with a wide range of toys—both masculine and feminine—tend to be better adjusted and more well-rounded than their gender-typed counterparts. They also tend to have a wider and more diverse skill set. When you look at playground behaviors, for example, boys are more likely than girls to run, jump, climb, and play ball. These behaviors help them with gross motor skills, which involve large muscle movement, strength, and coordination. Girls, on the other hand, more often gravitate to things like jump rope, hopscotch, chalk art, string games, and clapping verses. Many of these activities tend to help them develop fine motor skills, which involves small movements involving the fingers, wrists, hands, and lips. All of these skills are important, and encouraging a wide range of play behaviors can help kids—both boys and girls—develop a wide range of skills and interests.

Toy companies have seized upon this challenge, particularly when it comes to creating toys that encourage girls to delve into the world of science, technology, engineering, and math (STEM). For example, GoldieBlox, a company that was launched from a Kickstarter campaign, creates building sets specifically aimed at girls. LittleBits, another start-up company, allows kids to create simple electronic devices using an open-source library of magnetically connected circuit boards. Roominate, a product pitched on the television show *Shark Tank*, is a home-building set that includes modular furniture and walls, as well as motors and light circuits. Even well-established companies are joining the party. The Lego company, for example, launched a very popular line called Lego Friends, specifically aimed at girls.

This is good stuff, right? Not so fast. All of these toys feature pastel colors and feminine princess-esque characters—subtle gender cues that could actually reinforce stereotypes. Moreover, all of these toys are pre-determined sets. A Lego Friends set, for example, only comes with the Lego pieces needed to build the set. The same is true for GoldieBlox. Because they're so tightly engineered, these sets don't really encourage open-ended play, and that could also result in unintentional stereotyping.

Now, take a look at this 1981 advertisement:

This Lego ad from 1981 resurfaced in 2014 as a challenge to today's Lego Friends line, which heavily features pink and is advertised specifically to girls. The 1981 ad, in contrast, refers to Legos as a "universal building set." The girl in the photo is all grown up now. Her name is Rachel Giordano, and she's a doctor.

In 1981, Legos weren't sold in predetermined sets. Neither were building toys like Tinkertoys, Magna-Tiles, and plain old building blocks. None of these toys are gender typed, and all of them encourage problem solving, social interaction, and creative expression. Sometimes, the simplest approach is the best!

FEMINIST HERSTORY: ROSIE THE RIVETER AND JUNE CLEAVER

Gender schemas don't appear out of nowhere. Lots of things influence our perception of gender over time. The media is one of the most powerful gender-socializing agents, and history is filled with examples.

Let's start with the World War II era. In many ways, war then was different than it is today. When a country went to war, it was a whole-country event—everyone was directly impacted by war, and everyone needed to contribute to the war effort in some way. Men went overseas to fight, creating a shortage of available workers. So the U.S. government stepped in and created a media campaign aimed at housewives, encouraging them to do their patriotic duty and enter the workforce. One advertisement said, "Longing won't bring him back sooner . . . Get a war job!" "Do the job he left behind!" said another. The song "Rosie the Riveter," recorded in 1942, used the story of a female assembly line worker to encourage women to join the workforce. That, of course, led to the iconic feminist image of Rosie the Riveter that is familiar to many of us. All of those media messages contributed to a very different cultural script about what it meant to be a woman.

This media campaign inspired a social movement across race and class lines. Since so many White and African-American women worked alongside each other, this war effort laid the groundwork for the Civil Rights movement. Unfortunately, when the war ended, the men came home, and the women were thanked for their service and told to go back into their homes. In order to ensure that women actually *would* go home (because many of them found fulfillment in the workplace and were reluctant to leave their jobs), the media was deployed once again. Beginning in the late 1940s and into the 1950s, stereotypes of the "happy housewife" saturated the media. Advertisements depicted women wearing dresses, heels, pearls, and classic hairstyles—and, of course, they wore a big smile as they vacuumed, cooked, and dusted. Television shows like *Leave it to Beaver, Ozzie and Harriet, The Donna Reed Show,* and *Father Knows Best* all depicted classic "family values," featuring White middle-class nuclear families with traditional gender roles, wives deferring to their husbands, and children learning moral lessons from their parents. These shows were entertaining, but they also prescribed what "normal" family life should look like.

Not surprisingly, these traditional gender schemas of the 1950s inspired the most popular toys of the era, and that, in turn, reinforced gender stereotypes among children. For boys, there were BB guns, Erector sets, Legos, and Tonka Trucks. For girls, there were dolls—Barbie, Chatty Cathy, and Raggedy Ann, to name a few. And guess what? There was also the Easy-Bake Oven.

TRY THIS!

Let's change a tire! Even if you don't have a driver's license or are too young to drive a car, knowing how to change a tire is a good skill to have. There's nothing worse than being stranded at the side of the road, waiting helplessly for someone to come to your rescue. Once you change a tire for the first time, you'll feel like you can change the world!

Equipment (look these up if you're not sure what they are!):

- Spare tire
- Tire jack
- Cross wrench (or cordless impact wrench)
- Tire blocks, bricks, or medium sized rocks

Directions:

- Make sure the car is parked on level ground, with the engine off and the parking brake on.
- If you have tire blocks, put them under the tires to keep the car in place. You can use rocks too.
- If your car has hubcaps, loosen the lug nuts—these are the nuts that keep the hubcap on. When you use the wrench, remember: lefty-loosey, righty-tighty. If the lug nuts are really tight, jump on the cross wrench. If you have a length of hollow pipe, attach that to the cross wrench for extra leverage. Or you can use WD-40 to loosen the lug nuts. If all else fails, try pouring Coca-Cola over the lug nuts. (If it's powerful enough to loosen stuck lug nuts, you might want to think twice about drinking it.) Don't take the lug nuts all the way off—just loosen them.
- Raise the car off the ground with the jack. All jacks work differently, so consult the instruction manual if you need to. Usually there's a solid metal plate on the car frame, in front of the back tire frame and just behind the front tire. Once you've found this, put the jack under the metal plate, and start pumping. The car will lift off the ground. Make sure the jack stays connected to the metal plate. Stop pumping when the car is six to eight inches off the ground.
- Remove the lug nuts, and put them somewhere safe. Grab the tire and pull it toward you.
- Pick up the spare tire and align its holes with the bolts. Push the spare onto the tire bolts until it stops completely. Replace the lug nuts and tighten, but not all the way.
- Carefully pump down the jack to lower the car, stopping when all four tires are back on the ground.
- Tighten the lug nuts. But don't go in a circle. Tighten the first, then tighten the one across from it, and continue from there.

Congratulations! You did it! Don't you feel like Supergirl? Now go teach your friends how to do it.

F IS FOR

FAMILY LIFE

Family Life—the most dreaded class of my sophomore year in high school. Miss Sanderson, one of the gym teachers, taught it—and from the very first day, you could tell that she would have rather been anywhere but there. *Anywhere.* She said all the right things, like:

"I'm always here if you need me."
"Ask any question you want."
"I want us to be as open and honest as possible."

But her body language and tone of voice said *Let's just get through this, okay?* No one asked questions. No one volunteered anecdotes. No one came to her after class for advice. Why would we? Despite what she said, she did not convey a welcoming, open attitude about the subject she was teaching.

That subject, of course, was sex education. And frankly, I didn't find it to be helpful at all. Giving a class a code name automatically sends the *no-real-talk-allowed-here* message, loud and clear. So we didn't talk about anything real. We weren't even open about the word "sex"! We were given tests with diagrams of male and female reproductive systems, and we had to identify and define each anatomical part. We memorized effectiveness rates of various contraceptive methods, but never learned how to use them. We viewed images of gross things growing from men's and women's genitals, but never talked about how to prevent that from happening. And this was in 1987, during the height of the AIDS crisis. The overall message that I got was: *Just don't do it. You'll be better off. Trust me.*

But since when does a teenager in Family Life class trust what their gym teacher (who really doesn't want to be there) is saying? If the teacher code was *no real talk allowed here*, the student code was *we're just going to do it anyway, but we'll adhere to the teacher code, and we won't talk about it.*

Today, when I ask my students what they learned in their sex education classes, I get a wide range of responses. Some of them never took sex ed, either because their schools didn't offer it, or because their parents pulled them out of class. Others got an unbelievably comprehensive education on the subject, arming them with as much information as possible. But the vast majority of my students had exactly the same experience I had. And this is almost 30 years later.

So many parents and teachers fear that if you tell kids about sex, then they're going to run right out and do it, but that's not the truth. In fact, when kids get accurate, comprehensive, and age-appropriate information about sex, they tend to make better decisions about sex—and, compared to those who receive no sex ed (or very poor-quality sex ed), they are much more likely to delay having sex. They also have lower rates of teenage pregnancy and STIs.

Feminists have been pushing for accurate, comprehensive, and relevant sex education for decades. They've also pioneered the concept of feminist sex-positivity. Instead of teaching girls, "You're going to get pregnant and die," feminist, sex-positive educators believe that sex is good, healthy, and natural—and, in order to make good decisions about sexual activity, we should be given as much information as possible.

Gayle Rubin was one of the first feminists to advocate for sex-positivity. In 1975, she wrote a groundbreaking essay titled "The Traffic in Women: Notes on the 'Political Economy' of Sex," which helped reframe the conversation about gender and sexuality. She became active in the BDSM (bondage, domination/submission, sadism/masochism) community in San Francisco, and through that involvement became a pro-sex activist. In 1984, Rubin wrote a now-classic article titled "Thinking Sex," which laid the foundation for feminist sex-positivity. Because of Rubin's work, we now have a wide range of contemporary feminist sex-positive activists, ranging from author Susie Bright to YouTube sex educator Laci Green.

What if all teachers (including Miss Sanderson) developed a sex-positive perspective? What if they learned how to talk about sex without feeling embarrassed, ashamed, or dirty? What if all of us could ask the questions we really wanted to ask, and get accurate, complete, and unapologetic answers? Imagine the possibilities.

FEMINIST HERSTORY: MARGARET SANGER

Let's go back to 1872. That year, a man named Anthony Comstock wrote a bill called the "Suppression of Trade in, and Circulation of, Obscene Literature and Articles of Immoral Use." He believed that contraceptives, among other things, promoted lewd, obscene, and lustful behaviors. In keeping with his beliefs, this bill made it illegal to send the following items through the U.S. mail: erotica, sex toys, letters with sexual content or information, contraceptives, and substances that induce abortion. The "Comstock Law" passed on March 3, 1873. About half of the states in the U.S. passed more stringent anti-obscenity laws, banning the advertisement, possession, and sale of "obscene" materials, including contraceptives. As recently as 1960, thirty states still had these kinds of laws on the books.

No one challenged these laws until 1916, when Margaret Sanger opened the first birth control clinic in the U.S. She believed that women should be able to make choices about their bodies, and they should be able to decide whether or not to have children. She also wanted to educate women about abortion and prevent back-alley abortions from occurring. All of this, from her perspective, was critical in the movement towards women's equality. Shortly thereafter, Sanger was arrested for distributing information about contraception—and the aftermath of her arrest and trial led to the modern reproductive rights movement. In 1921, Sanger founded the American Birth Control League, which changed its name to Planned Parenthood in 1942. Planned Parenthood operates clinics throughout the United States, providing a wide range of reproductive health care services and information to girls and women.

Although Margaret Sanger was a leader in the women's movement, she is a controversial figure. She opposed discrimination against African-Americans and publicly expressed acceptance of homosexuality. She strongly opposed censorship, as she was arrested numerous times for speaking in public about contraception in places where that kind of speech was illegal. However, she also opposed sexual "indulgence." She was repulsed by masturbation, believing that it was unsafe. And many considered Sanger's role in the African-American community to have a racist agenda. She opened a birth control clinic in Harlem and later participated in the Negro Project, which distributed birth control to poor African-American communities. While some view this as a form of outreach, others have criticized Sanger, suspecting that her ultimate goal was to reduce the Black population. Sanger also supported the practice of eugenics, which refers to a set of practices that prevent childbirth among the "unfit," including immigrants, poor people, and the "profoundly retarded." All of this has made poor communities of color reluctant to join the reproductive rights movement, which has been a source of tension among feminists.

In 1965, the Supreme Court decision *Griswold v. Connecticut* legalized birth control in the United States. A year later, Margaret Sanger died at the age of 86 of congestive heart failure.

TRY THIS!

We're going to design a sex education lesson! But before we do that, here are a few questions to think about:

Have you taken a course in sex education? Was it called "Sex Education," or was it called something else? If it was called something else, why do you think that was the case?

What did you learn in that class? On a scale from 1–10 (1 being lowest, 10 being highest):

- How open and honest were the discussions in class?
- How useful was the information that was presented?
- What sexual values did you learn? Were they communicated openly, or were the messages more subtle?

Now, think about these questions:

- What did you want to know or learn that you didn't? What questions do you still have?
- Where, besides sex ed class, have you gotten information about sexuality?
- What sexual values do you think are important for teens to learn?

Okay. Now that you've answered these questions, let's start creating an awesome sex ed lesson! Make a list of all the topics you think are important to include. Then select one of those topics. This is going to be the focus of your lesson.

Collect as much information as you can about that topic. Look for sources of information that you can trust. Planned Parenthood's website is a good place to start. There are also lots of Internet resources for teens, including Scarleteen (www.scarleteen.com); Sex, Etc. (www.sexetc.org); and Laci Green's YouTube channel.

Now that you're an expert, what do you think is the best way to teach this topic? You could ask students to act in skits, participate in role-plays, create art, play a game—the possibilities are endless. Be creative!

IS FOR

GEEK

One day after school, my daughter had a play date at her friend Mari's house. When I came to pick her up, Mari's older sister Sydney was just coming home. We started chatting. "Why did you stay after school?" I asked.

"I was at Minecraft Club," she said. "I love Minecraft." She smiled and cocked her head. "I'm *such* a geek."

I could relate—sort of. I was a different kind of geek when I was her age, but a geek nonetheless. My head was constantly buried in a book. Math was my favorite subject; solving geometric proofs and factoring polynomials was my idea of fun. (Truly.) Sydney is a gamer geek; I was a book and math geek.

But here's the big difference between Sydney and me. I *never* would have called myself a geek. NEVER. If anything, I did everything in my power to avoid being called a geek. Geeks were the outcasts, the rejects, the lowest of the low. Sydney, on the other hand, wasn't embarrassed or ashamed at all. When Sydney called herself a geek, her voice was confident and her body language was strong. In fact, she brandished that word like a gleaming sword, ready to swashbuckle her way through the world of Minecraft. "Geek" was a badge of honor.

My approach was to avoid the word "geek" like the plague. Sydney's approach was to own it unapologetically. When people reclaim words that were originally used in hurtful ways, they're engaging in something called *re-appropriation*. You see this a lot in groups that have been historically oppressed. For example, the word "queer" has historically been used as a slur against gay men, but lately, the LGBT (lesbian, gay, bisexual, transgender) community has taken back that word and used it in positive ways to describe themselves. Some feminists use the word "girl" as a term of empowerment rather than as a diminutive term that cuts women down to size. ("Girl power!" might be an example.) Re-appropriation allows oppressed communities to *own* words, so that those words can't be used to hurt them again.

Like Sydney, more girls and women are embracing male-dominated "geeky" pursuits such as gaming, math, science, computers, comics, and science fiction. Girls sometimes have a hard time breaking into "geek culture," and when they do, they might experience some pushback from boys. "Fake geek girls" is an example. These are (theoretically) groupies trying to look cool, trying to find a boyfriend, or tagging along behind their boyfriend. And they have no "geek cred," at least according to boy-geek-culture standards.

Because of that, a number of women have established safe, empowering spaces for girls to engage in geek activities. Let's talk about two of them.

Kimberly Bryant is the founder of an organization called Black Girls Code, which offers workshops, hackathons, and after-school programs that encourage girls from underrepresented groups to develop computer programming skills. Bryant, an electrical engineer, understands the cultural isolation and self-doubt that often results from the lack of African-American role models and peers in her field. And employment data validates her experience—most tech companies have an embarrassing lack of diversity. One survey of major tech companies like Google, Facebook, and Apple showed that the overwhelming majority of those in technology jobs and leadership positions were White and Asian-American males. In contrast, only 7% of those in leadership positions and 8.5% of those in technology jobs are women who identify as something other than those two ethnic groups, including African-American, Latinx, Native American, and mixed-race individuals. While Bryant's program itself teaches African-American girls how to code, the overarching goal is to change the face of the tech industry, while bridging the digital divide—the gap between those who have reliable access to technology and those who don't.

Here's another example. Lala Castro and Tanya Salcido are the co-founders of #LatinaGeeks, a website that brings information about the tech world to Latina women. The two co-founders, both of whom have a long history of involvement in the tech, marketing, and social media worlds, realized at some point the absence of Latina girls and women in geeky spaces. At events and conferences, for example, there was often only a handful of women—and *no* Latina women—who expressed an interest in technology. Recognizing that digital divide brought Lala and Tanya together to create #LatinaGeeks. It creates Latina visibility by profiling women gamers, techies, and math-lovers, among other things, and it aims to bring more Latina girls and women into the world of geek.

Because of cultural re-appropriation—the positive reclaiming of the word "geek"—geek girls can be proud of who they are. And as the number of community spaces and role models for geeks increases, geek girls don't need to stay in hiding anymore.

FEMINIST HERSTORY: *WIMMEN'S COMIX*

The 1930s to the early 1950s was the Golden Age of Comic Books. You're probably familiar with the comic book characters introduced during this era: Superman, Batman, Wonder Woman, Captain America, and Catwoman, to name a few. The comic book world was heavily dominated by males, from the characters themselves to the cartoonists all the way up to the comic book sellers. Not only that, classic comics were notorious for their stereotypical depictions of women and the sexualization of female superheroes.

Then, in 1954, the Comics Code Authority (CCA) ushered in a new era. Modeled after the Hollywood Production Code of the 1950s, the CCA forbade depictions of sex, violence, drugs, or anything socially progressive. From that point forward, all comic book content had to be reviewed by the CCA before receiving a stamp of approval. Only then could they be released for sale in mainstream stores.

These conservative (some would say "regressive") policies gave rise to an underground "comix" movement, which began to gain momentum in the late 1960s. Instead of the stereotypical "hero rescuing the damsel in distress" stories, these underground comix contained blatant portrayals of sexuality, drug use, and violence. This movement, led by artists like Robert Crumb ("R. Crumb") and Gary Panter, sold their work in head shops and other black market outlets, creating popularity within the counterculture scene while staying under the CCA's radar.

Radical and socially progressive stuff, right? Not so much when it came to feminism. Instead, images of naked women being raped, tortured, degraded, and murdered filled the pages of these comix. For the most part, men were the cartoonists, and women were the objects of their work. The few women who did speak out were dismissed; "You're being too sensitive," or "You have no sense of humor" were typical responses.

Trina Robbins, one of the few female comic book artists active then, was sick of it. She had discovered a Berkeley-based feminist publication, *It Ain't Me, Babe*, that awakened her to the realities of sexism. From that point forward, Robbins couldn't *not see* sexism, particularly within the comic book world. She began drawing comics for the newspaper, and in 1970, she and co-creator Barbara "Willy" Mendes published an offshoot comic book with the same title—the first all-women's feminist comic. Like the fan fiction of today, the comic took familiar characters ranging from Olive Oyl to Wonder Woman, this time breaking out of their stereotypical roles and fighting against the *patriarchy* (a word that refers to a system of male power and domination). Two years later, Robbins and nine other women published the first issue of *Wimmen's Comix*, featuring a story about an out lesbian titled "Sandy Comes Out."

Wimmen's Comix functioned very differently than most male-dominated comic book publishers. Instead of a hierarchical structure where power rested at the top, it relied on a model of shared power. The organization was managed as a collective, with rotating editors in collaboration with one another. Artists with no cartooning or illustration experience were encouraged to contribute. It didn't matter that some drawings looked amateurish; the goal was to give women a voice in the comic book world. And it did, tackling subjects like abortion, female sexuality, lesbians, and feminist politics.

After seventeen issues, *Wimmen's Comix* went out of print in 1992, but the spirit of feminism in the comic book world lives on. Although there is still no shortage of oversexualized depictions of women in comics, there's plenty of countermessaging out there too. From comic strips like Alison Bechdel's *Dykes to Watch*

This cover is from the first issue of *Wimmen's Comix*, titled "Sandy Comes Out." It marked the first time that openly lesbian relationships were depicted in the comic book world. *Credit: Wimmen's Comix #1* (1972), cover art by Patricia Moodian

Out For, to political 'zines like the 1990s Riot Grrrl publications, to graphic novels like Bechdel's wildly popular *Fun Home*, comics have been a powerful weapon in the feminist superpower arsenal.

TRY THIS!

What's the absolute worst thing that someone could call you? Why? Take a few minutes and write about how being called that name or label makes you feel.

Have you ever been called a name that made you uncomfortable, or that hurt your feelings? How did you handle it?

Now, let's play with cultural re-appropriation. What happens when you call yourself that name, in the most confident and loving voice possible? Can you identify anything positive about that name? For example, if someone called you "weird," is there anything about being weird that you could take pride in and feel good about?

H IS FOR

HERO(INE)

"My hero!"

That's the last line in many fairy tales, comics, and love stories, right? Action movie plots frequently revolve around the "girl needing to be rescued." Many classic fairy tales involve a girl being saved by a Prince Charming—Cinderella, Snow White, and Rapunzel, to name just a few. Even in *Star Wars*, Princess Leia utters her famous plea: "Help me, Obi-wan Kenobi! You're my only hope!" The hero saves the damsel in distress, and they live "happily ever after."

Of course, the "happily ever after" part of the story trails off into the sunset, leaving the details up to the imagination. But since when do fairy tales come true?

Many people think that chivalry is a way of treating women with respect. Holding a door open for her, paying for her meal on a date, giving up his seat for a girl or woman—boys often learn to do these things as a form of politeness. But really, all of these supposedly noble acts are what's known as *benevolent sexism*. When a man engages in chivalrous behaviors towards women, it often feels flattering (hence the term "benevolent"). *What a nice man!* women often think to themselves. But the assumption behind his behavior is that women are fragile and delicate beings in need of a man's protection and care. (That's the "sexism" part of the equation.) He is the hero, and she is dependent on him. Does that sound like equality to you?

A perfect example of this happened to me: One morning in one of my classes, I couldn't get the video equipment to work properly. After trying a couple of things that didn't work, and then pausing a moment to consider my next action, two male students jumped up in an attempt to "come to the rescue." While I'm grateful that they got the equipment to work in relatively short order, there was something about the incident that just felt wrong. It could be read as two students being polite and helpful, or it could be read as the knights in shining armor coming to rescue the helpless princess. That's the "my hero!" phenomenon.

So why get all upset about knights coming to the rescue, if it ultimately gets the video equipment up and running? Let's talk about some tangible gender inequalities that coexist with benevolent sexism:

- In countries where the "my hero!" attitude is more common, men live longer than women, men are better educated and have higher literacy rates, and men have more purchasing power than women.
- People who value the "my hero!" attitude are less likely to have positive attitudes towards lesbian, gay, and bisexual relationships.
- People who value the "my hero!" attitude are more likely to have negative reactions towards femininity in males.
- People who value the "my hero!" attitude are more likely to encourage *heterosexism*—the assumption that everyone is

heterosexual, that heterosexuality is the "normal" way to be, and that women belong with men.

- People who value the "my hero!" attitude are more likely to be transphobic.

So, let's recap. Benevolent sexism is dangerous because it is linked to gender inequities and because of its association with homophobia, heterosexism, and transphobia. But one of the most dangerous things about benevolent sexism is that many girls and women don't view it as sexism; in fact, they may find it to be quite palatable. And once they drink the proverbial Kool-Aid, they're more likely to find other forms of gender-related oppression—such as homophobia and transphobia—to be acceptable as well.

That doesn't mean that a male shouldn't ever hold a door open for a female. If she's right behind him, holding the door would be the kind thing to do, right? And if the person walking behind him happens to be male, he should hold the door open for him too. If a female is in front of a male, and she gets to the door first, she should hold the door open. The point is to recognize benevolent sexism and to understand that girls and women don't need help and protection because they're female. However, recognizing when we truly need help, accepting it when help is offered, and being willing to help others when they need it, regardless of gender—*that's* a much more empowered place to be.

FEMINIST HERSTORY: THE STORY OF FA MU LAN

Boy meets girl.
Boy falls for girl.
Boy saves girl . . . and they live happily ever after.

Fairy tales, contemporary novels, movies—"boy saves girl" is one of the most common narratives in storytelling. But not all heroes are boys, and not all girls need to be saved. Take Fa Mu Lan, a story about a Chinese girl who became a warrior in order to defend China from being invaded. From "The Ballad of Mulan," a poem first transcribed in the sixth century, to the contemporary Disney film *Mulan*, the story of Fa Mu Lan has been told and re-told for centuries.

In many ways, the story told in *Mulan* is quite different from the original, and some people have challenged the accuracy of the Disney adaptation. While those criticisms are fair, it's important to understand that many ancient legends weren't written down. Instead, they were shared through the *oral tradition*, in which information was passed down from one generation to the next through spoken word. Ways of sharing ideas, knowledge, spiritual beliefs, and cultural material included songs, riddles, prayers, legends, chants, proverbs, nursery rhymes, and performances. The story of Fa Mu Lan was told for centuries before anyone actually wrote it down, so there are lots of variations on the story.

In general, here's how the story goes: Mulan lived during the Northern Wei Dynasty, which was a time of intense political and cultural change. When she was seven years old, Mulan began training to be a woman warrior. She knew how to ride a horse and use a sword, and she practiced archery and martial arts. Then, China was invaded by the Mongols and by nomadic tribes, and each family was expected to provide one family member, typically a boy, to go to battle. Mulan's brother was very young, and her father was too old to fight. So Mulan disguised herself as a man and joined the army in her father's place. After twelve years of fighting, she was offered twelve ranks, but she turned them down, resumed her female persona, and returned home to live a peaceful life. Because of her bravery, Mulan inspired many other young women to practice the skills of a woman warrior.

Let's fast-forward to the 20th century and meet a Chinese-American feminist writer named Maxine Hong Kingston. She was born in Stockton, California in 1940, shortly after her mother came to the U.S. from China. As a young girl, Kingston wanted to be a writer. The first article she ever wrote, titled "I Am an American," won a prize and was published in *Girl Scout Magazine*. Later, she went to UC Berkeley and majored in English. In 1976, Kingston wrote her first book, titled *The Woman Warrior: Memoirs of a Girlhood Among Ghosts*. In this book, Kingston blends the story of her childhood with retellings of ancient Chinese legends, including the story of Fa Mu Lan. She begins her story like this:

> *When we Chinese girls listened to the adults' talk-story, we learned that we failed if we grew up to be but wives or slaves. We could be heroines, swordswomen.*

Through the story of Fa Mu Lan, Kingston learned that girls and women could (and should) be powerful, that they could protect their families and fight for justice. Maybe she could become a woman warrior too! But, as Kingston soon found out, this fantastical story of a woman warrior clashed with the stark reality of being a Chinese-American girl in the 1940s and 1950s. Let's look at a few passages from *The Woman Warrior*, and you'll see how confusing it was to be a girl living between two cultural worlds:

> *There is a Chinese word for the female I—which is "slave." Break the women with their own tongues!*
> *I went away to college—Berkeley in the sixties—and studied, and I marched to change the world, but I did not turn into a boy.*
> *"Bad girl," my mother yelled, and sometimes that made me gloat rather than cry. Isn't a bad girl almost a boy?*

The Fa Mu Lan story was incredibly inspiring to Kingston. But it didn't match her lived experience. Because:

- How can a girl become a warrior if the female *I* in Chinese means "slave"?
- Fa Mu Lan marched into battle too, and she changed the world. Why wasn't Kingston awarded twelve ranks for her bravery?
- If being a girl is so unacceptable, would being a "bad girl" make her a boy? Would that make her more acceptable?

These are the contradictions that so many girls and women face in our society. But we all have an inner Fa Mu Lan—a warrior woman who is willing to fight for what's right and just. Maxine Hong Kingston recognized that, and she used the legend of Fa Mu Lan as a vision of empowerment. You too can be a hero!

TRY THIS!

Many books and movies, both classic and contemporary, involve a male "hero" who rescues a female or otherwise "saves the day." Fairy tales, in particular, tend to rely on the "hero" storyline. And yet, some of the best fairy tale retellings involve "flipping the script"—in other words, the same story is told from a different point of view. Marissa Meyer has done this brilliantly in *The Lunar Chronicles* series (*Cinder, Scarlet, Cress, Fairest,* and *Winter*), as well as in books like *Heartless*, the Alice in Wonderland story with the Queen of Hearts centered as the main character. Another example is the Broadway play *Wicked*, which tells the story of the Wizard of Oz from the perspective of the Wicked Witch. When the same story is told from a different point of view, new insights begin to emerge, particularly when it comes to playing with gender.

Now it's your turn! Choose a book or movie that you know well and that fits this description. Then write that same story, but from a different point of view. What happens, for example, when a Superman movie is told from Lois Lane's point of view? Or if one of the *Star Wars* movies is told from Princess Leia's point of view?

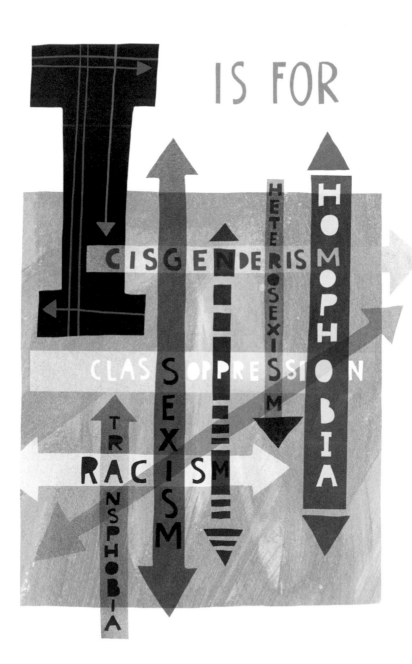

IS FOR

I

CISGENDERISM
HETEROSEXISM
HOMOPHOBIA
CLASS OPPRESSION
TRANSPHOBIA
SEXISM
RACISM

INTERSECTIONALITY

Most feminist must-read book lists include *The Feminine Mystique* by Betty Friedan. Released in 1963, *The Feminine Mystique* addressed "the problem that has no name"—the widespread unhappiness and despair among housewives in the 1950s and 1960s. Throughout the book, Friedan addresses the role of the media in creating this "feminine mystique"—this glorified image of the happy housewife—while sharing stories of women whose lives have been completely unfulfilled by this role. According to Friedan, feminists have fought hard for the right to an education and a good career, and the only way to overcome the "feminine mystique" is to pursue education and meaningful work. In 1966, Friedan co-founded and became the first president of the National Organization for Women (NOW), one of the largest and most well-known liberal feminist organizations in the United States. Many believe that the publication of *The Feminine Mystique* and the establishment of NOW are what launched the second wave of feminism.

That same year (1963), Dolores Huerta and Cesar Chavez founded the United Farm Workers Union, which fought for higher wages, better working conditions, and immigrant rights for agricultural workers, the majority of whom were Mexican or Filipino. Around the same time, Phyllis Lyon and Del Martin founded the Daughters of Bilitis (DOB), the first national lesbian social and political organization in the United States. Later that year, Martin Luther King, Jr., gave his famous "I Have a Dream" speech, which galvanized the African-American civil rights movement.

Even in the midst of these overlapping social movements, *The Feminine Mystique* focused only on middle-class, educated White women, assuming that their plight was the plight of all women. It didn't address any of the issues commonly faced by women of color, poor women, lesbian women, working women, and immigrant women. In fact, at times throughout her life, Betty Friedan was openly hostile to certain groups of women, famously referring to lesbians as "the lavender menace." If Friedan had taken an intersectional approach to feminism, her book would have looked a lot different.

What does that mean, "an intersectional approach to feminism"? Let's use the example of an African-American lesbian woman. She might be seen for her "gayness" within the LGBTQ community, for her "blackness" within the African-American community, and for her "femaleness" when she's involved with a women's group. But you can't split off different aspects of a person's experience; people come in a whole package, and that package is comprised of a wide range of overlapping identities. When we take an intersectional approach, we're going beyond a split-personality concept of identity, because compartmentalizing different parts of our identities is limiting and oppressive. Moreover, an intersectional approach addresses the interconnectedness of racism, sexism, homophobia, and class oppression, calling for the dismantling of the "system" of oppressions.

Betty Friedan isn't the first to take a non-intersectional view of women and feminism. During the early 1900s, when women were fighting for the right to vote, many suffragettes argued that if White women won the right to vote, that would help suppress the political power of African-Americans. Carrie Chapman Catt, who founded the League of Women Voters, said this: "White supremacy will be strengthened, not weakened, by women's suffrage." And Elizabeth Cady Stanton, a famous suffragette, said, "What will we and our daughters suffer if these degraded black men are allowed to have the rights that would make them even worse than our Saxon fathers?"

Here's another example. In 1973, feminist leader Robin Morgan had some choice words regarding transgender women: "I will not call a male 'she'; thirty-two years of suffering in this androcentric society, and of surviving, have earned me the title 'woman'; one walk down the street by a male transvestite, five minutes of his being hassled (which he may enjoy), and then he dares, he dares to think he understands our pain? No, in our mothers' names and in our own, we must not call him sister."

Despite the oppression women have experienced within mainstream feminism, women have found many ways to insert themselves into the movement. Some have fought to create a place at the table alongside White women. Others have created their own branches of feminism. Womanism, for example, focuses on the experiences of African-American women. *Mujeristas* are Latina feminists, who address issues like immigration, religion, and family, as well as gender roles. Queer and trans feminism (discussed later in this book) takes up the needs of sexual and gender minorities. All of these approaches involve taking an intersectional approach to feminism.

Imagine how different our school history lessons would be if the textbooks utilized an intersectional feminist lens. Here's an example: Many kids learn at some point about Elizabeth Cady Stanton's and Susan B. Anthony's contributions to the suffrage movement. But most of us never learned about Ida B. Wells. She was born a slave in 1862, just before the Emancipation Proclamation. When she was a young adult, a train conductor told her to give up her seat in the first class ladies' section and move to the smoking car. She refused—71 years before Rosa Parks did the same thing on a bus in Montgomery, Alabama. She became an investigative journalist and a leader in the anti-lynching campaign. But she, like Elizabeth Cady Stanton and Susan B. Anthony, was also a suffragette, and was committed to social justice for women. Unfortunately, Ida B. Wells' contributions to the suffrage movement aren't typically included in history books. Ida had many sides to her identity, and intersectional feminism helps to illustrate those connections. When we don't use an intersectional lens, we tend to view people as one-dimensional—and a one-dimensional view never adequately addresses oppression.

FEMINIST HERSTORY: THE COMBAHEE RIVER COLLECTIVE AND *THIS BRIDGE CALLED MY BACK*

> *We are a collective of Black feminists who have been meeting together since 1974. [1] During that time we have been involved in the process of defining and clarifying our politics, while at the same time doing political work within our own group and in coalition with other progressive organizations and movements. The most general statement of our politics at the present time would be that we are actively committed to struggling against racial, sexual, heterosexual, and class oppression, and see as our particular task the development of integrated analysis and practice based upon the fact that the major systems of oppression are interlocking. The synthesis of these oppressions creates the conditions of our lives. As Black women we see Black feminism as the logical political movement to combat the manifold and simultaneous oppressions that all women of color face.*

This statement was written by the Combahee River Collective, an organization founded in 1974 by Black feminists and lesbians in Boston, Massachusetts. The Collective's name references the Combahee River Raid, a resistance action led by Harriet Tubman that freed more than 750 slaves. The group began as an offshoot of the National Black Feminist Organization (NBFO) to organize in response to two sources of frustration: racism and marginalization within the White feminist movement; and sexism within the civil rights, black nationalism, and Black Panther movements. These founding members knew from the beginning that their platform would centralize issues of racial, sexual, heterosexual, and class oppression, marking a distinctly intersectional approach.

In 1977, three members—Demita Frazier, Beverly Smith, and Barbara Smith—co-authored the Combahee River Collective Statement. Twin sisters Beverly and Barbara had been working at *Ms.* magazine, which provoked backlash from White feminists and from Black male activists. In this document, they highlighted a number of critical ideas:

- The concept of multiple, interlocking oppressions;
- The importance of challenging racial and sexual oppression;
- The role of capitalism, cultural imperialism (the practice of imposing cultural standards onto a less powerful group), and patriarchy;
- The challenges Black women faced in their activist efforts, including lack of time and money, family responsibilities, and fatigue from dealing with multiple oppressions.

Although the Combahee River Collective disbanded in 1980, other feminists of color picked up where they left off. In 1981, Chicana feminists Cherríe Moraga and Gloria Anzaldúa released an anthology titled *This Bridge Called My Back: Writings by Radical Women of Color*. Grounded in intersectional feminism, *This Bridge Called My Back* brought the experiences of women of color to the forefront, while issuing a call to action for White feminists to support and empower them. In addition to the original Combahee River

Collective Statement, *This Bridge Called My Back* included several now-classic pieces, including the following:

- Audre Lorde's famous essay titled "The Master's Tools Will Never Dismantle the Master's House," where she argued that ignoring race as a feminist issue ends up reinforcing patriarchy;
- Gloria Anzaldúa's "La Prieta," a powerful account of her childhood where she compared herself to a Shiva, "a many-armed and legged body with one foot on brown soil, one on white, one in straight society, one in the gay world, the man's world, the women's, one limb in the literary world, another in the working class, the socialist, and the occult worlds."
- A poem by Chrystos titled "I Walk in the History of My People," an evocative piece that addresses genocide, colonization, poverty, and the reservation system. Chrystos, a member of the Menominee tribe, identifies as a lesbian and as Two-Spirit, a term used in many Native communities to signify a non-binary or shifting gender identity.

Both the Combahee River Collective Statement and *This Bridge Called My Back* set the tone for a more inclusive, intersectional, and grassroots feminism. They are considered to be required reading for feminists today.

TRY THIS!

For this exercise, you'll need:

- 20 index cards
- a pen

Take each index card and write "I am" on the front. Leave some room to write more on the card. Then, go back through the stack of cards, and complete the sentence by writing down one of your identities. For example, you might have cards that say, "I am female," "I am an immigrant," "I am Jewish," "I am Black," or "I am trans." These are just examples—everyone has a different collection of identities, and yours will be unique to you.

Now, take the stack of cards, and arrange them in order of "most important identity" to "least important identity." When you finish that task, answer these questions:

- What are your top 5 identity cards? Why are they so important to you?
- How easy or difficult was it to rank-order your identity cards? Which identity cards were easy to rank, and which ones were harder?
- Did any of your rankings surprise you? Why?

Now, we'll do this exercise again, but with a twist. Instead of rank-ordering your identity cards, spread them out in front of you, and arrange them in a way that best represents how your identities shape who you are. You could create a circle, or you could allow identity cards to overlap, or you could have multiple circles. Or you can do something else entirely! It's completely up to you—these are your identities, and you're the one who best understands how they influence your life.

What did you come up with? Was this easier or harder than rank-ordering your identity cards?

IS FOR

JOKE

"What's the difference between trash and a Jersey girl?"
"Trash gets picked up."

I'm originally from New Jersey. As a teenager, I heard this joke All. The. Time. Usually I just sighed and rolled my eyes. But once in a while, I'd speak up. "That's so rude!" I'd say. Or "That's so sexist!" Whenever I said something, whoever told the joke would typically make a comeback like: "Wow, you're so uptight! Can't you take a joke?" Or he might say to his friends, "She must be on the rag!"

Even though feminism has made enormous strides in the last few decades, girls and women are still subjected to these kinds of jokes. And it's often hard to hold the joke-teller accountable for their sexism. If you speak up and voice your opinion, one way the joke-teller might evade responsibility is to throw criticism your way. It's very effective, actually, because the problem ceases to be the joke. Now *you're* the problem—because you're so sensitive, or so uptight, or you have no sense of humor.

Sidestepping responsibility for sexism becomes even easier when the offending behaviors are more subtle. For example, Vera, who is 10 years old, loves outdoor play. Getting dirty doesn't bother her in the least, and she'd rather run around with the boys at recess than hang out with the girls. One day when they were playing kickball, her friend Lucas said, "You're really good—for a girl."

Lucas thought he was paying Vera a compliment, but he was, in fact, expressing a sexist attitude—that girls, by definition, aren't good at sports. Now Vera is in a double-bind. If she accepts Lucas's compliment, she's also quietly endorsing his sexist attitude. However, if she challenges Lucas's statement, Vera runs the risk of coming off as rude and unappreciative.

These subtle expressions of sexism are what psychologists and other researchers call *microaggressions*. Other forms of oppression, such as racism and homophobia, can be revealed through micro-aggressions as well. For example, Marta, who is Latina and has lived her whole life in Oregon, often gets asked, "Where are you from?" When she says, "Oregon," the inevitable follow-up question is, "No, where are you *really* from?" Microaggressions are where unconscious attitudes tend to leak out—attitudes like "Latinas must all be from Mexico" or "Girls aren't good at sports."

So, can you call out sexism, or racism, or homophobia, or any other form of oppression, and still have a sense of humor? Of course! There are lots of ways to be funny. Jokes don't have to involve cutting someone else down.

Here are some questions to think about:

- Have you ever experienced a microaggression? Give an example.
- Was it based on your gender, your race or ethnicity, your sexual orientation, or something else?

- How did you respond to the microaggression? How could you respond differently?
- How did you feel when the comment was made?
- Have you ever engaged in microaggressive behaviors without realizing it? Now that you know what a microaggression is, how might you act differently in the future?

FEMINIST HERSTORY: THE POLITICS OF "GOOD HAIR"

"Daddy, how come I don't have good hair?"

When three-year-old Lola asked this question, her father, the famous comedian Chris Rock, didn't know what to say. But it was clear that Lola had already bought into the idea that kinky, curly Black hair was not "good hair." It's easy to see why, considering the frequency of microaggressions against African-American hair:

- In 2012, while Gabby Douglas was busy winning gold in both the individual all-around and team competitions (she was the first American gymnast to do this, by the way), the Internet was busy exploding with nasty comments about her hair.
- In 2014, a Florida school threatened to expel a 12-year-old girl because her natural hairstyle was a "distraction" to the other students.
- In 2016, Gabby Douglas returned to the Olympics—and so did the hateful comments about her hair.

Clearly, Lola's question didn't come out of nowhere. But where did these ideas of "good hair" and "bad hair" come from?

Africa is a diverse continent, and with that diversity comes a wide variety of African hair types. Historically, hairstyles throughout Africa have often been quite intricate, with braids, twists, curls, and adornments such as shells, beads, or strips of cloth. You could learn a lot about a person just by looking at their hair. Hairstyles communicated information about a person's age, ethnic identity, religion, marital status (or availability for courting), clan or tribe membership, wealth, and status in the community. In many communities, if a woman's hair was unclean, undone, neglected, or otherwise messy, something must have been terribly wrong with her. And because hair carried such value throughout Africa, hairdressers were highly respected and trusted members of the community.

Let's rewind all the way back to the 1400s. The slave trade, which lasted for almost four hundred years, changed everything. About twenty million Africans, mostly between the ages of ten and twenty-four, were forcibly removed from their homes and sold to slave traders from Europe. After they were sold, their heads were shaved, which was a powerful way of stripping them of their African cultural identity. This also marked the beginning of the devaluation of African hair. When their hair grew back, slaves didn't have the time or materials to maintain their hair. They combed their hair with sheep carding tools, and they resorted to using bacon grease and kerosene to straighten their hair. Often they just wrapped their heads with a scarf or kerchief. House slaves, on the other hand, were expected to look clean and well-kept, so they were allowed to wear cornrows or tight braids. Soon, the idea of "good hair" vs. "bad hair" began to take hold—slaves who had light skin and straight hair commanded higher prices at auction, and Blacks began to internalize the idea that dark skin and kinky hair were unattractive.

Then the Civil War ended, and the slaves were free. However, if Blacks wanted to achieve the American Dream—and if they wanted to help elevate their race as a whole—they needed to look as "White" as possible. Newspaper and catalogue advertisements reinforced this message; one 1923 ad for Golden Brown Beauty Preparations stated, "Pride in our race demands that we look light, bright, and attractive." Another ad, this one for Madam C. J. Walker's

Hair and Toilet Preparations, said, "From A Slave Cabin to Riches and a Benefactress to Her Race" and emphasized that readers, too, could have "luxurious hair" and a "flawless complexion." (Walker, by the way, was the first female self-made millionaire in America.)

Later, "good hair" shifted from being an aspirational goal to an actual requirement. Let's use churches as an example. In some White neighborhoods, churches had a brown paper bag and a fine-toothed comb hanging outside the front door. If a person's skin was darker than the brown paper bag, or if the comb couldn't get through a person's hair, then that person would not be allowed inside. Variations of these "tests" were used in schools, nightclubs, fraternities and sororities, and business networks to keep dark-skinned, kinky-haired African-Americans out.

During the Civil Rights movement in the 1960s, the Afro hairstyle emerged as a symbol of Black pride and resistance. This image was powerfully embodied in the famous FBI Wanted poster of Angela Davis. A wider range of images that embraced Black hair began to emerge, featuring cornrows, dreadlocks, and head wraps. Meanwhile, the African-American hair care industry still continued to capitalize on products like the hot comb, the Jheri curl, chemical relaxers, and weaves, all of which tamed the kinks, curls, and locs that are natural features of African-American hair.

Let's go back to three-year-old Lola. Her question was loaded, that's for sure. But learning more about the history of Black hair in America helps us to understand where all these microaggressions came from. But here's the bigger question: How do we move away from Black hair being such a target for microaggressions? Let's look at a few examples:

- **Education.** In order to combat oppression, you have to know the history behind it. When she was a student at Barnard

On these two pages is an advertisement for Madam C. J. Walker's Preparations. Madam C. J. Walker was the first female self-made millionaire in the United States. Although she was enormously successful, her success rested upon convincing African American women that beauty involved having straight hair and a light complexion. *Credit:* Collection of the Smithsonian National Museum of African American History and Culture, Gift of A'Lelia Bundles / Madam Walker Family Archives

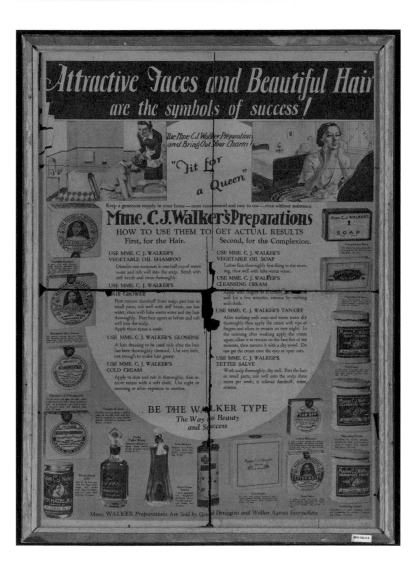

INTERSTATE FLIGHT - MURDER, KIDNAPING
ANGELA YVONNE DAVIS

FBI No. 867,615 G

Photograph taken 1969   Photograph taken 1970

Alias: "Tamu"

DESCRIPTION

Age:	26, born January 26, 1944, Birmingham, Alabama		
Height:	5'8"	**Eyes:**	Brown
Weight:	145 pounds	**Complexion:**	Light brown
Build:	Slender	**Race:**	Negro
Hair:	Black	**Nationality:**	American
Occupation:	Teacher		
Scars and Marks:	Small scars on both knees		

Fingerprint Classification: 4 M 5 Ua 6
1 17 U

CAUTION

ANGELA DAVIS IS WANTED ON KIDNAPING AND MURDER CHARGES GROWING OUT OF AN ABDUCTION AND SHOOTING IN MARIN COUNTY, CALIFORNIA, ON AUGUST 7, 1970. SHE ALLEGEDLY HAS PURCHASED SEVERAL GUNS IN THE PAST. CONSIDER POSSIBLY ARMED AND DANGEROUS.

A Federal warrant was issued on August 15, 1970, at San Francisco, California, charging Davis with unlawful interstate flight to avoid prosecution for murder and kidnaping (Title 18, U. S. Code, Section 1073).

IF YOU HAVE ANY INFORMATION CONCERNING THIS PERSON, PLEASE NOTIFY ME OR CONTACT YOUR LOCAL FBI OFFICE. TELEPHONE NUMBERS AND ADDRESSES OF ALL FBI OFFICES LISTED ON BACK.

DIRECTOR
FEDERAL BUREAU OF INVESTIGATION

Entered NCIC
Wanted Flyer 457
August 18, 1970

UNITED STATES DEPARTMENT OF JUSTICE
WASHINGTON, D. C. 20535
TELEPHONE, NATIONAL 8-7117

This poster was created after FBI Director J. Edgar Hoover included Angela Davis on the Ten Most Wanted Fugitives List. Her bodyguard, Jonathan Jackson, used guns registered in her name in a Marin County courtroom kidnapping that resulted in the death of four people, including himself and the presiding judge. Angela was incarcerated for sixteen months, much of it in solitary confinement, before she was bailed out and eventually found not guilty. *Credit:* Collection of the Smithsonian National Museum of African American History and Culture

College, Ayana D. Byrd made Black hair the focus of her honors project. Later, she and journalism professor Lori L. Tharps expanded this project and co-authored a book titled *Hair Story: Untangling the Roots of Black Hair in America,* which provides an in-depth exploration of the role of Black hair in African-American history.

- **Entertainment (and Education).** Chris Rock didn't have an immediate answer for his daughter Lola. But her question got him thinking about "good hair" and "bad hair," which ultimately led to the production of his documentary film, *Good Hair.* Using his trademark edgy humor, Rock unpacks the $500 billion African-American hair industry and looks at how attitudes about Black hair act as a reflection of racism in America.

- **Empowerment.** Joey Mazzarino, a writer for the children's show *Sesame Street,* watched his young daughter Segi, who was adopted from Ethiopia, long for blonde hair that she could swing around. To challenge this and help her to embrace her hair, Mazzarino wrote a song titled, "I Love My Hair," which aired on *Sesame Street* for the first time on October 4, 2010.

TRY THIS!

Have you ever visited an art museum? If so, you've probably seen signs that say "PLEASE DO NOT TOUCH THE ART." Feminists and other social justice activists, however, have used art as a form of political expression, often inviting people to engage directly with the artwork by touching it, adding to it, or defacing it. It doesn't matter if the art is changed or destroyed in the process because participation is part of the art itself.

Let's look at some examples of participatory public art. The "Who Needs Feminism" campaign was a social media photo campaign launched by a group of students at Duke University. They prompted participants with the phrase, "I need feminism because . . ." and then asked people to create a sign completing the phrase and post it on social media. Another form of participatory public art is the "Before I Die" project, which invites people to reflect on issues of life and death, as well as share insights on how to live life to the fullest. "Before I Die" installations feature a large mural-sized chalkboard with the prompt, "Before I die, I want to. . . ." Participants are invited to take a piece of chalk and complete the sentence. Similarly, in "The Race Card" project, people are asked to take an index card and write six words that capture their thoughts, experiences, and observations about race, and are then invited to tack their cards on a public bulletin board for others to read.

Now, let's make an art project of our own! Create a participatory public art project, either by yourself or with friends, that educates people about sexist microaggressions. Come up with a name for your project that's catchy and memorable. You could model your project after one of the examples above, or you could do something entirely different. Be creative! You can start with a small group of friends or family members, or you can ask permission to do a large-scale event at your school or in your community. As you're creating this project, think about the following questions:

- What is the goal of your project? What do you want people to learn from it?
- What form of creative expression do you think would be most effective in conveying your message? Why?

- Participatory public art can sometimes lead to a backlash. For example, some responded to the "Who Needs Feminism" campaign by creating signs that said, "I DON'T need feminism because . . ." If vandalism, negativity, or some other type of backlash happens, how will you respond to it? Will you take action directly, or will you let the public participants respond?

K IS FOR

KNITTING

"When I was 13 my mother and aunt taught me how to knit. Ever since then I've grown a passion for it. But I never told anyone about it because I was afraid people would criticize me for doing something that seems 'boring' or 'not for my age.'"

A student in my Psychology of Women class wrote this in the margins of one of her tests. And frankly, it hooked me more than her response to the test question did. *Boring? Really?* I thought. When I was her age, I LOVED knitting—and embroidery, and sewing, and generally any fiber-related craft. I still love these things, but I could relate. When I was about her age, I didn't tell anyone either.

Why? Let's explore this a bit.

Decades ago, girls—but not boys—were always required to take home economics courses. Then, Title IX was signed into law in 1972 and everything changed. Title IX says:

> *No person in the United States shall, on the basis of sex, be excluded from participation in, be denied the benefits of, or be subjected to discrimination under any education program or activity receiving federal financial assistance.*

87

Essentially, what the law says is that girls and boys should have equal access to educational opportunities. So when I was in middle school, girls took wood shop, drafting, and computer classes alongside the boys, and boys took sewing and cooking classes with the girls. This was equality. And it was a good thing. Largely because of Title IX (and other feminist achievements), I had a broad-based public school education. I played sports. I took home economics courses. I went to college, and then to graduate school. In contrast, my grandmother, who in 1925 was privileged enough to attend college, was allowed to major in one of two things: teacher education or home economics. When you compare the options available to women today, it's obvious we've come a long way, baby.

But over time, schools stopped teaching sewing, and cooking, and home economics courses in general. Why? Because they're now seen as frivolous. It's traditional women's work—and modern women just don't do that sort of thing. This viewpoint—that modern, liberated women shouldn't have to learn those skills—is dangerous, in my opinion, and downright sexist, because it equates *feminine* with *bad*.

Knitting is not bad. Cooking is not bad. Learning how to clean your house, iron your shirts, develop a household budget, sew a button—none of these are bad things. They are, however, part of a feminine gender schema (remember that term?). In a society that loves to categorize things into boxes, all of these activities tend to go in the feminine box. If we're banishing the feminine, and telling girls (and boys) that these feminine pursuits are frivolous, unimportant, and unnecessary, we're contributing to a very dangerous cultural climate.

FEMINIST HERSTORY: DEBBIE STOLLER AND "GIRLIE FEMINISM"

Debbie Stoller was what I call a "Title IX kid." As a child of the 1960s and 1970s, she never had the experience of living in a world without feminism. Because of Title IX, which prohibited sex discrimination in education, she could play sports, take classes in math and science, and have legal protection against sexual harassment. She was surrounded by a culture of feminism, where she learned that she could do anything she wanted to.

But underneath that spirit of feminist empowerment, there was a powerful meta-message: If a girl wanted to knit and sew, she was squandering her talents and wasting her time. Instead, she should learn carpentry, play basketball, or join the science club. She should dream of becoming an astronaut, a neurosurgeon, or the President of the United States. If she spent her time doing traditionally feminine activities, she'd be doomed to a life of domesticity, which was everything feminism was fighting against.

So Debbie put down her yarn and knitting needles, and she became a card-carrying feminist. She went to Yale University and earned a master's degree in psychobiology and a PhD in the psychology of women. In 1993, Debbie and two other women launched *BUST*, a women's magazine that was intended to be a feminist alternative to *Vogue*, *Cosmopolitan*, and *Glamour*. *BUST* was grounded in the tradition of third-wave feminism—a grassroots movement and philosophical shift that incorporated issues of race, class, gender, and sexuality much more visibly than other waves of feminism. But all this time, Debbie secretly missed the fiber arts. Whenever she knitted, embroidered, or sewed, she felt connected to the women in her family. Eventually, she took up these activities again, but she did them in secret, fearing that the feminist police would take away her membership card if they saw her engaging in such domestic frivolity.

Finally, Debbie had an epiphany: Why is it cool for girls to engage in a traditionally masculine activity, but it's super-uncool for her to do something that's traditionally feminine? Why are knitting and sewing, both of which require math skills, spatial abilities, coordination, and focus, so devalued compared to, say, woodworking, which requires similar skills? She thought about her mother, her grandmother, her great-grandmother—the long line of women in her family who knitted and sewed—and she realized that *this* is why those activities got such a bad rap. They were traditionally done by women, which was enough to put those activities in the feminist no-fly zone.

So Debbie decided she wanted to "take back the knit." She used *BUST* as a platform, publishing articles about the importance of reclaiming and re-appropriating traditionally feminine activities—along with patterns for knitted bikinis and skull-patterned sweaters. She made knitting more visible by knitting in public and organizing "Stitch 'n Bitch" sessions (which later served as the title for her wildly popular book series). She popularized the concept of "girlie feminism," a term originally coined by Jennifer Baumgardner and Amy Richards in their 2000 book *Manifesta: Young Women, Feminism, and the Future*. Girlie feminism, as part of the third-wave movement, involved validating traditionally female activities, valuing women's work, embracing sexual experimentation and feminine expression, and respecting the history of women in the world of crafting.

TRY THIS!

Let's play with embroidery! Don't panic—embroidery is one of the easiest things to learn, even if you don't know how to do anything with fabric or thread or yarn.

First, you'll need some supplies. You can find all of these at your local crafts store.

- An embroidery hoop
- Needles

- Embroidery floss
- Scissors
- Fabric (plain cotton works well)
- Iron and ironing board
- Pencil

Think of a word or phrase you'd like to embroider. It could be simple, like a single word. Or it could be a quote, or an entire manifesto! For this example, I'll use "BOYS CAN SEW," although you can choose whatever you want. (Yes, boys can sew! If you're a boy, and you've never done embroidery, give it a try!)

Cut a square of fabric that's slightly larger than your embroidery hoop. Iron the fabric so it's nice and smooth. Then take your pencil and lightly write the word or phrase you want to embroider.

Now, let's put the fabric in the hoop. Separate the two hoops, then lay the inside hoop (the smaller one) on your table. Lay your fabric over the inside hoop. Now place the larger hoop on top. It'll look like an embroidery hoop sandwich, with the two hoops on the outside, and the fabric in the middle. Once you've done that, push the two hoops together, then tighten the screw and pull the fabric so it's taut.

Now it's time to embroider! Embroidery floss comes in six strands—you can use all six strands at once for a thicker stitch, or you can use two or three strands for a finer, more detailed effect. Whatever you decide, take a nice long piece of embroidery floss and thread it through your needle. Then tie a knot at the opposite end of the strand.

We're going to learn how to do the backstitch. This stitch is easy, and it works really well for text.

Start at the top of the letter "B." Poke the needle through the fabric from back to front, then pull the floss all the way through until the knot stops at the fabric. Now, make a stitch that's about a quarter of an inch long—poke the needle through the fabric from front to back, then pull it taut. YAY! You've made your first stitch!

Here's where it gets fun. Poke the needle through from back to front about a quarter-inch from the previous stitch, and pull the floss through. Now, poke the needle from front to back through the hole you made from your first stitch, and pull the floss through. Now you have two stitches that are joined together, with no gap in between. Cool, huh?

Keep doing this over and over until you're done!

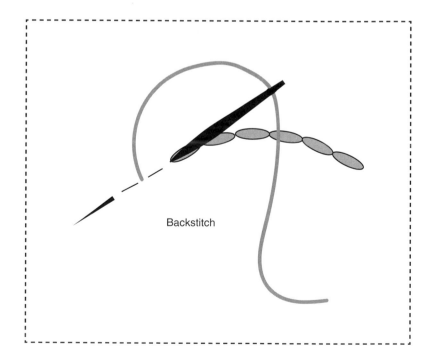

Backstitch

There's a lot you can do with a simple backstitch. But if you want to take your embroidery skills to the next level, the possibilities are endless! There's satin stitch, seed stitch, feather stitch, chain stitch, lazy daisies, and my personal favorite, the French knot. Once you master some basic embroidery stitches, you can stitch up all sorts of fabulous feminist messages.

L IS FOR

#BOYS READ GIRLS

Malala Yousafzai

LITERACY

That powerful headline was the title of an article written by Christina Hoff Sommers for *TIME* magazine. Sommers, whose article was based on her book *The War Against Boys: How Misguided Policies Are Harming Our Young Men*, believes we've all bought into "the myth of shortchanged girls"—the idea that girls face invisible gender obstacles at school that prevent them from succeeding. In fact, according to Sommers, it's the opposite—*boys* are the ones whose aspirations and abilities are being crushed. Their grades are falling. They read less than girls do. Their college enrollment rates are dropping. They're more likely than girls to be suspended from school, and they have higher dropout rates. They are more prone to receiving a diagnosis of attention-deficit hyperactivity disorder (ADHD). The list goes on and on.

Why is that? Sommers' argument first appeared in her controversial 1994 book, *Who Stole Feminism? How Women Have Betrayed Women*. In this book, Sommers challenges what she calls "gender feminism," which calls for eliminating sexism by dismantling male supremacy, and argues in favor of "equity feminism," which seeks equal rights for women and men. (As an aside, "gender feminism" and "equity feminism" are probably a re-branding of *radical feminism* and *liberal feminism*, respectively.) Six years later, in *The War Against Boys*, Sommers takes this argument a step further and applies it to the educational environment. Because of gender feminism, says Sommers, schools have become more and more "girly" (or *feminized*, to use a more academic term), creating a hostile learning environment for boys. The result? Poor learning outcomes, increased social problems, and a higher likelihood of getting into legal trouble.

These are all serious allegations, but let's back up and focus on just one area of concern: reading. The phrase "reluctant reader" has gained considerable traction in the world of education, and boys are more likely than girls to receive this label. Mo Willems, the author of the popular Pigeon books and a reluctant reader himself, even went so far as to say, "'Reluctant reader' is code word for 'boy.'" Why that's the case is unclear. Maybe boys can't sit still long enough to read. Maybe boys would rather be playing outside and doing something physical. Maybe there aren't enough books that appeal to boys. Maybe boys *do* read, but what they read, like comic books and graphic novels, "doesn't count." Whatever the reason, we know this much: being a reluctant reader can be the start of a vicious cycle.

Scary, huh? Now, let's examine the research a little more deeply. According to the Brookings Institution's Brown Center on Education Policy, gender gaps *do* exist in reading and in math. Although girls lag behind boys in math achievement, they're ahead when it comes to the reading gap—and they have been since the 1940s. However, there's more to the story. Over time, the reading

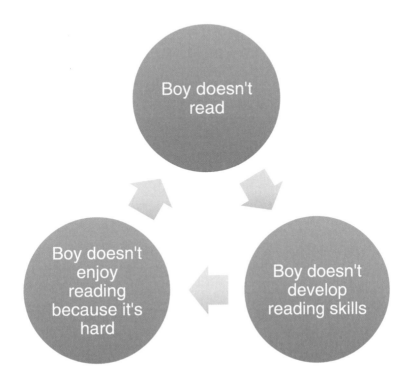

gap has become narrower . . . mostly. When we look at children from middle- and upper-income families, we see almost no gap in reading skills, and we see similar levels of overall academic achievement. However, the gap stubbornly persists among children in low-income families. Boys who are raised in low-income environments—*these* are the children who are most likely to be given the "reluctant reader" label.

Recently, I read an article written by Matt de la Peña, the Newbery-award winning author of *Last Stop on Market Street*, *Ball Don't Lie*, and *Mexican WhiteBoy*—and a former reluctant reader.

(So many famous authors were once reluctant readers!) Consider what he had to say about his own childhood and reading:

> *I didn't read a novel all the way through until after high school. Blasphemy, I know. I'm an author now. Books and words are my world. But back then I was too caught up in playing ball and running with the fellas. Guys who read books—especially for pleasure—were soft. Sensitive. And if there was one thing a guy couldn't be in my machista, Mexican family, it was sensitive.*

A "machista" is a man with an exaggerated sense of masculinity. It's a strong cultural value among many Mexican-Americans. And if machistas think that books are girly, then getting them to read is going to be a hard sell. Because this, ultimately, is what happens:

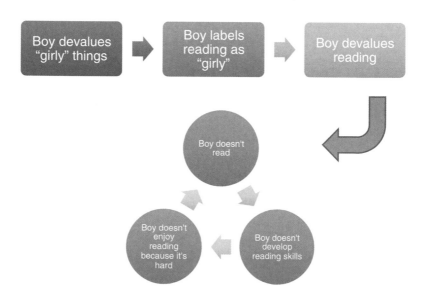

When you look at it from this perspective, it's clear that schools haven't become hostile to boys. Rather, if boys learn to fear the feminine, they're going to resist anything that's considered to be "girly." Even if it's good for them—like reading.

FEMINIST HERSTORY: LITERACY THROUGHOUT HISTORY AND AROUND THE WORLD

> *"A well-read woman is a dangerous creature."*
> —Lisa Kleypas, *New York Times* bestselling author

So dangerous, in fact, that some are willing to resort to violence to keep girls and women from becoming literate and educated. Consider the powerful story of Malala Yousafzai, a Pakistani teenager who became an activist for female education at age 11. (You're never too young to become an activist!) Under Taliban rule, girls were prohibited from going to school, and girls' schools were being closed by the Taliban military. Malala began blogging under a pseudonym about her experience, and she became more involved in educational activism. Her stories had a powerful effect on people, and her activism helped change educational policies. In 2012, while Malala was boarding a school bus, someone shot her (she survived, and is even more involved in activism around the world today). That's how much some people want to prevent girls from getting an education.

Throughout human history, people have gone to great lengths to prevent girls and women from reading. Despite the fact that the earliest author in recorded history was a woman (Princess Enheduanna of Mesopotamia, in 2300 B.C.), literacy among girls and women has been viewed as a powerful threat to patriarchal rule. In ancient times, reading and writing were strictly forbidden for girls and women. The written word was thought to have magical qualities, and the idea of a woman engaging in that way with written material was terrifying. In fact, the vast majority of people back then (both male and female) were illiterate, and only members of the religious elite could read or act as a scribe. Because most people were unable to read and write, scribes were responsible for reading things to common people. This was a very powerful way of keeping women in their place—if you think about it, depending on someone else to read written information to you robs you of the opportunity to think and reason independently.

All of this changed in the ninth century A.D., when Charlemagne, the first Holy Roman Emperor, championed literacy for both men and women. Charlemagne believed that teaching the larger population to read was important and necessary for an organized, cohesive society. This, as you might imagine, had a tremendous impact on women's literacy, and a literate class grew out of that movement. Even with that, women readers were still relegated to second-class status. Because girls and women weren't taught Latin back then, they couldn't read the Bible and other spiritual texts—the "gold standard" of reading materials at the time. They could, however, read books that were written in the common language that was easily understood—books that were considered to be of "lesser status" by men. In other words, yesterday's vernacular writing is today's "chick lit"—books that most men wouldn't be caught dead reading.

Literacy among girls and women has ebbed and flowed since then. In the 16th century, for example, reading was completely taboo for women, so instead of dispensing with reading altogether, they read in secret. The "pocket novel," which were smaller, cheaper versions of books that women could hide from their husbands, became wildly popular during this time. Later, during the rise of the Industrial Revolution in the 18th and 19th centuries, the concept of "separate spheres" for women emerged, and an opposite trend kicked in. For the first time, at least among middle- and upper-class families, men went off to work in factories, and women were expected to be keepers of the home. This coincided with the rise of the novel, which appealed especially to wealthy women who were part of this new "leisure class." This was the era that gave rise to authors like Charlotte and Emily Brontë, Louisa May Alcott, and Jane Austen, to name a few. Fiction became extremely popular during this era, particularly among women. But women were still urged to practice their reading habits in moderation. Some Victorian-era medical experts believed that reading was hazardous to a woman's health, potentially causing "the vapours," which could involve anything from breathing difficulties to emotional instability.

Now, it's silly to think of reading as the cause of psychological difficulties. If anything, reading and writing have demonstrated positive psychological effects (think bibliotherapy and journal-writing, for example). But even today, girls and women are still prevented from learning to read and write. Literacy rates have been increasing steadily over time, which is a good thing, but the vast majority of those who are illiterate are girls and women. According to the UNESCO Institute for Statistics, 477 million women worldwide cannot read or write. To give some perspective, there are currently about 320 million people living in the U.S. Imagine if our whole country—plus another 150 million or so people—couldn't read or write? Unconscionable.

So why are illiteracy rates so high, particularly among girls and women? The lowest literacy rates are in sub-Saharan Africa, South Asia, and West Asia—areas that tend to have high poverty rates, soaring population rates, and negative attitudes towards girls and women. Many villages and towns in rural areas don't have schools, and those that do lack basic facilities, like desks, books, lighting, and other supplies. Poverty and overpopulation are factors as well; in places where the population is soaring and resources are diminishing, poor people with large families often send their children to work in factories or mines. Some countries are controlled by corrupt politicians who line their pockets with money intended for schools. And in some places, gender bias prevents girls and women from pursuing their education. Clearly, there is still a fear of educated women, and some countries have bans on reading and education for girls and women.

Why is that? Why is there such a pervasive, worldwide fear of literate girls and women? Because reading is power. If women can read alone, without the guidance or help of a scribe, then they could learn to think independently. They might stop being compliant. Learning to read has been a powerful tool for women, because it's allowed them to become more aware of injustices against them. Not surprisingly, once women started becoming literate, they became more involved in protests against misogyny. Reading has allowed women to envision a different life for themselves, and to take action steps towards that vision.

TRY THIS!

Children's book publishers often say that girls will read anything, but boys won't read about girls. As a result, titles often get labeled as "boy books" or "girl books," and then marketed to those respective populations. And what ends up happening? Boys read "boy books," and girls read "girl books." It creates a literary gender divide that might not have existed in the first place.

What is a "boy book" and a "girl book"? How do you think publishers decide which categories books belong to?

Do you think boys should just read "boy books," and girls should stick with "girl books"? Why or why not?

Now, check out the #BoysReadGirls campaign on social media. You can use that hashtag on Twitter, Facebook, or Instagram. If you're a boy, answer this question:

Which books featuring girl characters do you love? Why? Now post your response on social media with the hashtag #BoysReadGirls.

Ask boys you know this same question. Encourage them to post their responses on social media as well.

MEDIA

"Mom, I'm not eating dinner tonight. I need to lose weight."

This is what eleven-year-old Sasha said to her mom. "Honey, why do you feel that way?" her mom asked.

"Because the kids at school say that I'm fat. One of them said that you're fat, too, and that her mom is skinny and pretty."

Our culture is saturated with toxic media which sends powerful messages to girls and women about how to be beautiful, sexy, flawless, and desirable for others (particularly for boys and men). Moreover, our culture is a chilly place for people whose bodies don't fit into the cultural ideal. Children who are overweight are more likely than their skinny counterparts to experience bullying. And adults who are fat are more likely to experience bias in health care, job discrimination, and other microaggressive acts. When the CEO of Abercrombie & Fitch says that the company won't sell plus-size clothing because they only want to target "cool, good-looking people," you know our culture has a long way to go when it comes to size acceptance.

Girls and women are subjected to even more rigid standards of beauty and attractiveness. Not only are girls and women judged on the basis of their appearance, but images of girls and women in the media are more likely to be sexualized. The lessons that are imparted by sexualized media messages include the following:

- You are valuable and worthy only if you are sexually appealing to males.
- You must be model-beautiful in order to be sexy.
- Your worth comes from being a sexual object, rather than from being intelligent, creative, or ambitious.
- Boys don't like girls who say "no."
- You are attractive only if you dress and act older than you are.

Sexualization occurs everywhere—TV, movies, song lyrics, music videos, the Internet, magazines, video games, sports media, and advertising. As our culture becomes more technologically advanced, it also becomes more media-saturated. And this saturation of sexualized content has steep consequences. According to the American Psychological Association Task Force on the Sexualization of Girls, continued exposure to sexualized media is associated with poorer school performance, low self-esteem, depression, eating disorders, risky sexual behaviors (no condom use, lack of assertiveness), stronger endorsement of stereotypes depicting women as sexual objects, and valuing appearance over other qualities.

So what can you do?

- You can learn to be critical of the media. Talk about what you're watching on TV, reading in magazines, or seeing in advertising. Challenge messages that you think are sexist or sexualizing.
- You can choose clothing that makes you feel comfortable. Develop your own sense of style. Dress for yourself, not for other people.

- You can speak up and take action if you see something that makes you uncomfortable. If you see a commercial that you think is inappropriate, write a letter to the company. If you read a magazine that sends sexualized messages to girls, stop reading that magazine. Choose to consume media that makes you feel good about yourself.
- You can do what you love. Get involved in activities that interest you, and you will meet others who share those interests.
- You can be you, and not try to model yourself after an unrealistic image.

FEMINIST HERSTORY: JEAN KILBOURNE AND MEDIA LITERACY

Like many of us, Jean Kilbourne had read many women's magazines, but had never really paid close attention to the advertisements. One day in 1968, while she was working at a job putting ads into a medical journal, she came across an advertisement that caught her attention. It said: "Ovulen 21 works the way a woman thinks—by weekdays, not by cycle days." The accompanying photo featured a woman with seven speech bubbles, each one representing a day of the week. Monday's "bubble" had a washtub, indicating that it was "washing day." Tuesday's "bubble" had an iron, so it was "ironing day"—and so forth. Kilbourne was struck by how sexist this ad was (especially because it was an ad for birth control pills!). She started to collect ads and put them on her refrigerator, and over time, she began to see patterns of sexism repeated again and again. She made slides of her images and started giving talks and presentations about women in advertising, which launched a national interest in media literacy and forced people to take advertising seriously.

This ad was featured in Jean Kilbourne's first film, *Killing Us Softly*. The overt sexism in this ad inspired Kilbourne to collect advertisements and view them with a more critical eye. *Credit:* Jean Kilbourne. "Killing Us Softly: Advertising's Image of Women." Northampton, MA: Media Education Foundation, 2010

In 1978, ten years after she saw that advertisement for Ovulen 21, Kilbourne made her first film, *Killing Us Softly*. In that film, Kilbourne shows how advertising reflects and reinforces our society's attitudes about girls and women. Examples in her first film included an ad for Love's Baby Soft, featuring a young girl made up to look older and seductive; an ad for flavored douches (really!) that invited women to "Come join the revolution!"; a deodorant ad that said, "Feminine odor is everyone's problem"; and an ad for shoes that said, "Keep her where she belongs." Since then, she has created three updates of her original film, the most recent being *Killing Us Softly 4: Advertising's Image of Women*. Kilbourne's other films, all of which put advertising under the cultural microscope, include

Pack of Lies; *Slim Hopes: Advertising & the Obsession with Thinness*; *Spin the Bottle: Sex, Lies & Alcohol* (with anti-violence educator Jackson Katz); and *Deadly Persuasion: The Advertising of Alcohol & Tobacco*. Her films have been incredibly popular with teen and young adult audiences, and her work has brought the link between media literacy and feminism to a much wider audience.

So, has advertising changed as a result of Kilbourne's work? In *Killing Us Softly 4*, Kilbourne begins with this sobering statement:

> *Sometimes people say to me, "You've been talking about this for 40 years, have things gotten any better?" And actually I have to say really they've gotten worse. Ads sell more than products. They sell values, they sell images, they sell concepts of love and sexuality, of success and perhaps most important—normalcy. To a great extent they tell us who we are and who we should be.*

Throughout the film, it's clear that things haven't gotten better. "People often accuse me of reading too much into ads," says Kilbourne in *Killing Us Softly 4*, pointing to a Burger King ad for the "Super Seven Incher." In the ad, a woman's mouth is open and ready to receive the, well, super seven incher. "I don't think I'm reading too much into this," Kilbourne contends. In modern-day ads, the models have become thinner, the link between femininity, sexuality, and violence is much more obvious, and the blatant sexuality often resembles pornography.

The good news is that more people are paying attention and speaking out. More brands are using real women as models. In 2012, *Seventeen* magazine declared a "Body Peace Treaty," stating that they would no longer Photoshop their images, and they would only feature real girls and healthy models. Countless girls and women have organized and engaged in activism against sexist advertising. One example is SPARK Movement, an organization that trains girls to become leaders in the feminist media literacy movement. And because of Jean Kilbourne's work, media literacy is a skill that is now commonly taught in schools. Slowly but surely, girls and women are changing the media landscape.

TRY THIS!

Studies have shown that girls and women who are regular readers of traditional women's magazines tend to feel more negatively about their bodies, compared to girls and women who don't read these magazines. Many of these magazines send damaging messages to girls and women about body image, sexuality, self-worth, attractiveness, and violence. Even with the surge of Internet use, women's magazines continue to be popular.

So . . . let's engage in some counter-messaging, and create a feminist magazine!

Before we start, take a few minutes to think about these questions:

- Who is your target audience? Do you want your magazine to appeal to people of all genders, or do you want to have a more specific focus?
- What information do you want to include in your magazine? Do you want to focus on politics, or style and fashion, or sports, or careers, or something else?
- What do you want your magazine to look like? Will it have a slick, professional look, or more of a DIY/zine style? Will you have a print version, an online version, or both?
- Who will be featured in your magazine? What images will readers see?
- Will you include advertising in your magazine? If so, think about what guidelines you might set with advertisers—lots of feminist publications do this.
- If you decide not to include advertising, how will you offset the costs of printing? Years ago, *Ms.* stopped including

advertisements in their magazine, which eliminated sexist images—but also drove up the cost of each issue.

Now, let's get to work on the first issue! Your magazine can be whatever you want it to be. If you have some ideas, then go for it! If you're stuck and not sure how to begin, here are a few guidelines:

- Choose a name for your magazine.
- Design the cover. What fonts will you use for the magazine title and other text? Will you use a photograph on the cover, or handmade art?
- You're the editor! Write a one-page "editor's note" that details the purpose of your magazine and what readers can expect to find as they read it.
- Ask your friends to write articles on specific topics you've chosen. Of course, you can write articles too! Or you can ask your friends to submit articles about feminist topics they've chosen.
- Include visuals in your magazine. Again, these could be photographs, drawings, paintings, graphic art—whatever you want! Make sure that the artwork speaks to the audience you're targeting.
- Play with the layout of your magazine. Look at magazines you enjoy reading, and identify things that are visually appealing to you. These could include colors, fonts or printing, and patterns as well as the overall page layout.
- If you have access to a scanner and a computer, scan each of your pages into the computer. Then, you can print them out and bind the pages together manually, or you can use word processing or desktop publishing software to create your magazine digitally.
- Share your magazine with others! Invite people to give feedback and to contribute to the magazine.

N IS FOR

NO!

If you want things to change, you have to speak up. Great advice, right? Except speaking up isn't always so easy. Especially since our culture is saturated with messages that tell girls and women the exact opposite. The Disney version of *The Little Mermaid* is a perfect example. Ariel, the main character, is a mermaid who falls in love with a human named Prince Eric. She makes a deal with Ursula the sea witch; in exchange for her voice, she can live as a human for three days. The only way she can get her voice back (and keep her legs) is if she can get Prince Eric to kiss her. This is a classic double-bind, and so many girls and women face it: You can have a voice, or you can have a man. Take your pick.

Now, most of us don't face such a stark dilemma, at least not in an obvious way. But there are lots of ways in which girls and women are rewarded for being quiet and unobtrusive, and punished for speaking up and speaking out.

Here's an example that shows how afraid women are of speaking up. Gina, a friend of mine who teaches self-defense, was leading a six-week class for teenagers. On the first day of class, she lined all the students up in a row, facing her. "We're going to practice saying NO," she said. "Say it loudly, and be confident."

Most of the girls giggled. Gina didn't miss a beat. "GO!" she said, pointing to Brittany, the first girl in line.

"No?"

"Are you asking a question?" said Gina playfully.

Brittany blushed. "I don't want to sound like a bitch."

And so it went, on down the line. Some girls said their NO loudly, clearly, and firmly. Others were more tentative. Afterwards, Gina asked them to sit in a circle, and the girls talked about what the exercise felt like. It was a fascinating conversation. They said things like:

> "I sound so rude when I say 'no' like that!"
> "I'd rather tone it down. I don't want to make a scene."
> "If I yelled NO!!! like that, I think I'd scare people!"

One girl said, "I've never said no like that before." She paused. "It felt kind of good."

Girls are often socialized to be nice, and to be considerate of other people's feelings. This isn't a bad thing—wouldn't the world be a better place if everyone could be considerate? However, girls often learn that being nice—and being liked, for that matter—are more important than being safe. So many girls don't want to upset people, or embarrass them, or overreact—and in some situations, that puts their physical and emotional safety at risk.

Saying "no" is empowering. But getting good at it takes some practice, and at first, it can feel clumsy and awkward. But the more you practice, the easier it gets. These guidelines are helpful to keep in mind:

- Practice sounding as confident and calm as you can—even if you don't *feel* calm. And even if your voice shook when you said "no," you can take pride in the fact that you said it. Here's a good example: When Maria Elena Salinas was first hired as a television reporter for Univision, she used to get stage fright, and her voice shook as she stumbled over her words. But she kept at it, and didn't give up. Now, she's one of the most famous news anchors in the Spanish-speaking community, and she's a strong advocate for the Latinx community.
- Get support from others. Jazz Jennings, a transgender teen who was labeled male at birth, knew at an early age that she was a girl. She wanted to share her story with others, and her parents supported her completely. The first few times she spoke publicly, she was really nervous. But lots of encouragement from her family helped Jazz continue to engage in public speaking. Now, Jazz speaks in front of audiences throughout the country, and she co-authored *I Am Jazz*, a children's book that shares her experiences.
- Make sure that your body language and tone of voice match your "no." For example, saying "no?" as a question, like Brittany did, makes it sound like your "no" is up for negotiation. Making a comment sound like a question, according to a number of studies, is much more common in girls than in boys. Linguists refer to that pattern as *upspeak*—where the last syllable? Of a word? Is spoken? With a higher inflection? Which often conveys a sense of uncertainty.

If you think about it, saying "no" is a way of setting a boundary for ourselves. But not everyone respects those boundaries. What if your "no" is challenged?

- Repeat yourself. Reinforce your boundary by saying "no" again.

- Stay focused. Don't get derailed by questions or challenges.
- Remember that "no" is a complete answer. Start off by being polite, of course. However, if your "no" isn't being respected, know that you don't need to apologize for your "no." And "no" requires no explanation.
- End the conversation if necessary. It's always your right to choose whether you want to participate in a conversation, or if you want to walk away from it.

FEMINIST HERSTORY: HOW WOMEN WERE SILENCED— AND RECLAIMED THEIR VOICES

Women's voices have been silenced throughout history. In fact, even in the earliest forms of government and legislation, which developed in Mesopotamia under the reign of Urukagina, King of Lagash (ca. 2350 BCE), there were laws passed that essentially legalized sexism. One of those laws regulated the number of husbands a woman could have; if a woman violated this law, she could be stoned to death. The other was a law that effectively silenced women. The original text of the law states: "If a woman says [text illegible in the original] to a man, her mouth is crushed with burnt bricks." Many modern historians believe that these two laws marked the earliest written evidence of the subjugation of women.

This kicked off a longstanding worldview that women should remain silent. We can see this in Homer's *Odyssey*, where Telemachus, the son of Odysseus and Penelope, says to his mother, "Mother, go back to your quarters, and take up your own work, the loom and the distaff . . . speech will be the business of men, all men, and of me most of all; for mine is the power in this household." In Sophocles' *Ajax*, the main character rebukes Tecmessa, who had been taken captive by him during the Trojan War, by saying, "Woman, to women silence is the best ornament." Greek philosophers took the silencing of women a step further; Plato believed that women were intellectually inferior to men, and Aristotle thought that women lacked the ability to reason, and therefore needed to remain obedient to men.

Then there's religion. In the *English Standard Version Bible*, Timothy 2:12 reads: "I do not permit a woman to teach or to exercise authority over a man; rather, she is to remain quiet." And 1 Corinthians 14:24 says: "The women should keep silent in the churches. For they are not permitted to speak, but should be in submission, as the Law also says." Whenever women have tried to challenge the system of male dominance within the clergy, this is the passage that's typically cited as a counter-argument. In many denominations, women are allowed to serve as pastors and other members of the clergy. However, the Catholic Church still forbids women from entering the priesthood, and there are some evangelical churches that forbid women from holding positions of power—particularly if they involve public speaking.

We can even see the impact of silencing women in the field of psychology. Consider the case of 15-year-old Dora, a patient of the famous psychoanalyst Sigmund Freud back in the early 1900s. Dora had been the victim of sexually inappropriate behavior by one of her father's male friends. Shortly after the incident, Dora began experiencing symptoms of a psychological disorder known at the time as *hysteria*, which was why her father took Dora to see Dr. Freud. Her main symptom? She lost her voice. As therapy progressed, Dora made the connection between the sexual violation she experienced and the loss of her voice—which makes sense, right? However, Freud didn't see it that way; he told Dora that the incident didn't really happen, and, to add insult to injury, that she was actually secretly attracted to her father's friend but couldn't admit it. She was "crying rape" but really wanted it anyway—that's essentially what Freud's response boiled down to. No wonder Dora lost her voice—it was taken away from her, multiple times.

How have women fought back against being silenced? To answer this, let's travel to the mid-1800s, when the women's suffrage movement started to gain traction. One of the early suffragettes was Lucy Stone, who went to Oberlin with the goal of becoming a women's rights lecturer. Although Oberlin was progressive for its time as the first college in the U.S. to admit both women and African-Americans, the institution did not allow women to speak in public. Hoping to gain some practical speaking experience, Stone enrolled in a college rhetoric class, but even there her options were limited. Women in the class served as the audience for their male classmates, and they were expected to learn through passive observation. For all its progressiveness, the centuries-old tradition of keeping women silent was alive and well at Oberlin.

Stone took matters into her own hands. She and her friend Antoinette Brown, who also wanted to learn public speaking, organized a secret society—an all-women's debating club. They held their meetings in the woods with a lookout stationed to stand watch. When the weather got too cold to meet outside, they met at the home of one of Lucy's African-American classmates. Her house was on the outskirts of the town, and the girls came one or two at a time to avoid attracting attention. Later, after several months of meeting in secret, Stone got her rhetoric professor to let them engage in debate in class, but afterwards the faculty board quickly implemented a ban on women's debate in coeducational classes.

Stone kept trying to assert her right to speak publicly at Oberlin, but her efforts were largely in vain. When she graduated from Oberlin in 1847, she was the first female college graduate from Massachusetts. And yet, Stone refused to write a commencement speech because she knew she wouldn't be allowed to read it. Ten years later, in 1857, Oberlin College finally allowed women to speak at a public ceremony or forum.

Meanwhile, Lucy Stone went on to become one of the most powerful female orators in history. She gave speeches and lectures throughout the United States, focusing on women's voting rights, abolitionism, and women's dress reform (in particular, abandoning tight-fitting bodices and corsets and instead wearing loose-fitting "bloomers"), among other things. When she married, she refused to take her husband's last name, which was a groundbreaking act for the time.

TRY THIS!

Saying no takes practice. And even then, there are some situations where it's really hard to say no. So let's start with something easy.

For one week, choose one thing every day that you wouldn't ordinarily say "no" to. It shouldn't be something big or important— it should just be something you usually say "yes" to. Then, instead of saying "yes," say "NO!"

For example, if a friend offers you a snack that isn't your favorite, but you usually accept it because you don't want to hurt your friend's feelings, try saying "no."

Or here's another example: Let's say you are going to the movies with your friends, and you don't usually care what you go see. This time, if the suggested movie isn't one you want to see, try saying "no." Then suggest a different movie.

Throughout the week, keep a journal of how you feel every time you say "no." At the end of the week, read over your entries. Did your feelings change over the course of the week? Did it get easier to say no the more you practiced? If it didn't get easier, consider doing this exercise for another week.

Strive for saying "no" without feeling guilty. Remember, you have a right to say "no" whenever you wish, and to feel good about doing so.

IS FOR

OPTIONS

In my Psychology of Women class, we had just finished watching one of Jean Kilbourne's *Killing Us Softly* films. We had a lively group discussion, focusing on the power of advertising, the ways in which female sexuality and violence are linked together, the effects of advertising on body image, and the increased sexualization of girls, among other things. Then, one student raised her hand.

"The woman who was speaking? She was wearing makeup. And she looked like she dyed her hair. How can she criticize the media and still do those things? She can't be a real feminist."

Then, another student jumped in.

"I think if she wants to wear makeup, that's her choice. Isn't feminism about having the freedom to choose?"

So. If you're a feminist, can you wear makeup? Can you go on a diet? Can you wear dresses and high heels, or shave your legs, or dye your hair? Was Jean Kilbourne exercising her freedom of choice, or was she selling out to "the Man"?

Lots of feminists would say that feminism is all about choice. Take liberal feminism, for example. Liberal feminists believe that women and men are equal and have the same capacities and abilities.

Because of that, women should have equal pay, equal job and educational opportunities, and equal representation in the political system. Everyone, according to liberal feminism, should have equal access to opportunities regardless of one's gender, and being female shouldn't limit their choices. Some people call this "choice feminism," which asserts that every time a woman makes a choice, she's exercising her personal agency, and that is a feminist act.

If a woman wants to wear makeup, or dye her hair, or wear a dress and high heels, that's her choice. We're allowed to make controversial choices, too. So if a woman wants to be a sex worker, like a stripper, exotic dancer, or prostitute, that's her choice.

But are all of our choices really *free* choices? If we go beyond the individual and look at the context in which these choices are made, it becomes easier to see how "choices" are potentially limited by structural inequalities. Take sex work, for example. Many feminists have fought hard to have sex work recognized as a legitimate job and career choice for women. A good example of this is depicted in the classic documentary film *Live! Nude! Girls! Unite!*, which shares the story of a group of strippers who formed a union to advocate for their workplace rights. Women have the right to fair wages, reasonable work hours, and a workplace free from sexual harassment.

So, from this perspective, sex work is a feminist choice that's potentially fun and empowering. However, there's another side to this. The majority of women in prostitution are poor women of color, many of whom have a history of sexual abuse. For these girls and women, sex work wasn't necessarily a free choice. Instead, they made that "choice" because there weren't any other options. Moreover, many girls and women in the sex industry have been trafficked, meaning that they were illegally traded into slavery. Clearly, this scenario doesn't involve free choice at all.

Let's go back to the makeup/hair dye/dress-and-high-heels issue. Can you be a feminist and still do these things?

You get to choose what to do with your body. I have a poster in my office titled HOW TO BE A FABULOUS FEMINIST, and it includes this statement: "Decorate your body any way you like." Your body is yours. No one else should have a say in what you choose to do with your body, unless you give them permission.

All of our choices have consequences. All of us should be free to choose what we want. However, our choices have consequences. When we wear makeup, we're contributing to a $55 billion industry that capitalizes on making girls and women feel bad about how they look. On the flip side, wearing makeup may make you look more culturally attractive, and more attractive people have an easier time getting a job, making more money, and finding relationships. Clearly, there isn't a *right* choice—but there is an *informed* choice. Knowing your options and their consequences makes it easier to make a choice that's right for you.

Real choice comes from eliminating structural barriers that women face. In order to address inequality and lack of choice, we need to dismantle structures that limit our options. Feminists consider the following to be extremely important options (or rights):

- The right to freedom.
- The right to participate freely in our political system.
- The right to an education, and a broad range of educational paths.
- The right to pursue whatever career path we desire.
- The right to choose how we want to take care of our bodies— whether it involves saying no to an uncomfortable social situation, or having a range of options if we're faced with an unexpected pregnancy.

FEMINIST HERSTORY: CHARLOTTE PERKINS GILMAN AND SOJOURNER TRUTH

Charlotte was having a difficult time. She worried about everything. She couldn't eat or sleep. Every day she seemed to have less and less energy. So her family brought her to the doctor for help.

Neurasthenia, he pronounced as the final diagnosis, and she was given the "rest cure." She was ordered to stay in her room, lie in bed, and not get up unless she needed to use the bathroom. But instead of getting better, she got worse—much worse. She became panicky. Her thoughts became catastrophic and she started hallucinating, seeing things in the wallpaper that didn't really exist.

This is a true story. "Charlotte" was Charlotte Perkins Gilman, a nineteenth-century writer. She told her story in the short novella *The Yellow Wallpaper.* If we considered her situation now, we'd recognize that Charlotte was experiencing depression. And today, we would never advise her to restrict her activities and sequester herself in her room. But back in the late 1800s, people thought that girls and women, particularly middle-class White women, were delicate and fragile. They also thought that things like reading books, going to school, or engaging in intellectually stimulating activities could cause women to become mentally ill. So if a girl or woman showed signs of anxiety or depression, doctors told them to dial back their physical and cerebral activity—all the way to zero. In so doing, females were effectively stripped of their options.

Not all women during that time period were considered to be fragile, though. African-American girls and women, in contrast, were expected to perform hard labor, even after the Emancipation Proclamation. Sojourner Truth, an abolitionist and women's rights activist, said the following in her famous speech, "Ain't I a Woman?"

> *That man over there says that women need to be helped into carriages and lifted over ditches, and to have the best place*

everywhere. Nobody ever helps me into carriages, or over mud-puddles, or gives me any best place! And ain't I a woman? Look at me! Look at my arm! I could have ploughed and planted, and gathered into barns, and no man could head me! And ain't I a woman? I could work as much and eat as much as a man—when I could get it—and bear the lash as well! And ain't I a woman? I have borne thirteen children, and seen them most all sold off to slavery, and when I cried out with my mother's grief, none but Jesus heard me! And ain't I a woman?

Although they came from very different backgrounds, Charlotte and Sojourner had one thing in common—their options were severely restricted, either because of their gender, their race, or both. One of the goals of feminism is to make sure girls and women have options—the right to make their own choices, rather than someone or something else making choices for them. Studying women's history is one important way of learning about how women have been treated—and what rights they have secured over time.

TRY THIS!

Make a list of all of the freedoms, rights, and options you enjoy. They can be broad and global, such as "I have the right to go to school," and they can be very specific, like "I have the right to decide what I want to eat for breakfast." Hopefully you are able to come up with a long list!

Now, make a list of all the freedoms, rights, and options you *wish* you had. Again, they can be broad or specific.

What is standing in the way of you exercising these options? Which roadblocks might you be able to remove, and which ones do you have little control over?

IS FOR

PRIVILEGE

"Make a list of all the things you do to keep yourself safe."

This is the question I ask my Psychology of Women students when we begin our unit on gender violence. My female students typically write furiously, creating fairly lengthy lists. My male students, particularly those who are heterosexual and cisgender (meaning, not transgender), spend little time writing, and more time thinking. After a few minutes, I ask them to share their lists.

> *I make sure I have my keys in my hand when I'm walking to my car.*
> *I always let someone know where I'm going to be.*
> *When I go out, I'm careful about what I wear, because I don't want to call unwanted attention to myself.*
> *I don't wear earbuds when I go running.*
> *I pay attention to my surroundings.*

Typically, when one woman shares what she does to keep herself safe, other women chime in and say, "I do that too!" We usually generate a pretty long list. By the end, there's at least one man in the class who says, "I had no idea women put so much energy into protecting themselves."

This reality isn't new to most girls and women. But for many boys and men, it comes as a surprise. The fact that it doesn't even occur to most males to adopt these safety strategies illustrates their gender privilege. Cisgender males have the privilege of not having to worry about being attacked because they are male. Females, in contrast, don't enjoy that privilege.

Gender privilege isn't the only example. People who have White privilege, for example, can go into a department store without being followed around by a security officer, or go to school knowing that they will learn about White role models in English, science, math, and history. People with heterosexual privilege don't have to worry about being mocked (or attacked) for holding hands with their significant other, or worry about being fired from their job for being lesbian, gay, or bisexual. People who are able-bodied don't have to think about whether their friend's house has stairs, or if a concert will have a sign language interpreter. These are all things that people who enjoy privilege take for granted.

There are two things about privilege that make it especially dangerous. First, these kinds of privileges are unearned. It's one thing to gain the privilege of going on an overnight trip with your friends because you've been trustworthy in the past. That's an earned privilege. People who have gender privilege, or White privilege, or heterosexual privilege didn't do anything to earn it. They just existed, and that was enough to grant these privileges.

Second, unearned privilege tends to be invisible to the person who has it. This is why my male students are so surprised by the "how I keep myself safe" lists generated by the female students. If you're not aware of the privileges you have, it's impossible to see how much easier life is compared to those without privilege, and that realization can be powerful.

Once males recognize that they have unearned gender privilege, some choose to ally with the feminist movement. "Can a male be a feminist?" some people ask. Yes! There are lots of ways!

- Speak up when someone tells a sexist joke, or treats a girl or woman in a sexist way.
- "Yield the floor." Studies show that males tend to speak up more in class than females do, and they clock more overall speaking time than females do. Sometimes *not* being the first to speak up allows female students more opportunities to speak.
- Refrain from commenting on a female's weight or appearance in a disparaging or sexualizing way.
- Support other males in challenging masculine norms.

FEMINIST HERSTORY: PEGGY McINTOSH AND WHITE PRIVILEGE

In 1979, the Wellesley Centers for Women hired a young White feminist professor named Peggy McIntosh. She had previously taught at an all-girls school, where she was required to teach an all-male curriculum. Later, after she earned a doctoral degree from Harvard University, McIntosh took teaching jobs at several universities, where she used radical methods to teach about women and gender. When she started her job at the Wellesley Centers for Women, she was asked to teach college and university faculty how to incorporate research about women into their curriculum. This was her skill set, and even though most of the faculty in these seminars were men, she thought they were "nice men" who would be open to this concept.

They were nice men, for sure. But they were not open to the concept.

"My syllabus is already too full."

"I can't add anything else. There are too many other things I need to cover."

"It's important to cover the foundational concepts. There isn't room for the soft stuff."

McIntosh heard the same excuses over and over again, which was enormously frustrating. *These aren't overt sexists*, she thought. *They're nice men. How can these nice men be so resistant?*

Then, McIntosh had an epiphany. She'd been reading essays written by Black women about how difficult it was for them to work with White women. *That can't be true*, McIntosh had thought to herself. *I'm a nice person, and so are lots of other White women I know!* Her epiphany was: White women could be nice, but they could also be resistant, oppressive, and difficult to work with—just like the men she was trying to work with in her seminars. White people have privilege, just like males have privilege—and it's hard for people who have privilege to see it.

This realization led McIntosh to write her groundbreaking article, "White Privilege and Male Privilege: A Personal Account of Coming to See Correspondences Through Work in Women's Studies." In this article, McIntosh, reflecting on her own personal experiences, listed forty-six advantages that are conferred upon her regularly because she is White. Through these examples, McIntosh drew several conclusions:

- There is a difference between earned and unearned privilege. Privileges that are granted merely because of your skin color, sexual orientation, or gender are unearned.
- Unearned privilege tends to be invisible to the people who have it, but absolutely visible to those who are denied those privileges.

- We can have privilege in some areas (such as our race or sexual orientation) but be denied it in other areas (such as our gender or class status).
- When our unearned invisible privilege becomes visible to us, we become "newly accountable," meaning that we have a responsibility to engage in anti-oppressive behaviors.
- Eliminating unearned privilege will, in turn, dismantle oppression.

By writing this article, McIntosh started a large-scale cultural conversation about privilege and its relationship to oppression. She also identified a clear parallel between gender oppression and racial oppression, and through that she issued a call to action:

> *Through Women's Studies work I have met very few men who are truly distressed about systemic, unearned male advantage and conferred dominance. And so one question for me and others like me is whether we will be like them, or whether we will get truly distressed, even outraged, about unearned race advantage and conferred dominance and if so, what we will do to lessen them.*

TRY THIS!

The following is the original list of forty-six statements in Peggy McIntosh's classic article. Read through each of these statements, then answer "yes" or "no" to each.

1. I can, if I wish, arrange to be in the company of people of my race most of the time.
2. I can avoid spending time with people whom I was trained to mistrust and who have learned to mistrust my kind or me.

3. If I should need to move, I can be pretty sure of renting or purchasing housing in an area which I can afford and in which I would want to live.

4. I can be reasonably sure that my neighbors in such a location will be neutral or pleasant to me.

5. I can go shopping alone most of the time, fairly well assured that I will not be followed or harassed by store detectives.

6. I can turn on the television or open to the front page of the paper and see people of my race widely and positively represented.

7. When I am told about our national heritage or about "civilization," I am shown that people of my color made it what it is.

8. I can be sure that my children will be given curricular materials that testify to the existence of their race.

9. If I want to, I can be pretty sure of finding a publisher for this piece on white privilege.

10. I can be fairly sure of having my voice heard in a group in which I am the only member of my race.

11. I can be casual about whether or not to listen to another woman's voice in a group in which she is the only member of her race.

12. I can go into a book shop and count on finding the writing of my race represented, into a supermarket and find the staple foods that fit with my cultural traditions, into a hairdresser's shop and find someone who can deal with my hair.

13. Whether I use checks, credit cards, or cash, I can count on my skin color not to work against the appearance that I am financially reliable.

14. I could arrange to protect our young children most of the time from people who might not like them.

15. I did not have to educate our children to be aware of systemic racism for their own daily physical protection.

16. I can be pretty sure that my children's teachers and employers will tolerate them if they fit school and workplace norms; my chief worries about them do not concern others' attitudes toward their race.

17. I can talk with my mouth full and not have people put this down to my color.

18. I can swear, or dress in secondhand clothes, or not answer letters, without having people attribute these choices to the bad morals, the poverty, or the illiteracy of my race.

19. I can speak in public to a powerful male group without putting my race on trial.

20. I can do well in a challenging situation without being called a credit to my race.

21. I am never asked to speak for all the people of my racial group.

22. I can remain oblivious to the language and customs of persons of color who constitute the world's majority without feeling in my culture any penalty for such oblivion.

23. I can criticize our government and talk about how much I fear its policies and behavior without being seen as a cultural outsider.

24. I can be reasonably sure that if I ask to talk to "the person in charge," I will be facing a person of my race.

25. If a traffic cop pulls me over or if the IRS audits my tax return, I can be sure I haven't been singled out because of my race.

26. I can easily buy posters, postcards, picture books, greeting cards, dolls, toys, and children's magazines featuring people of my race.

27. I can go home from most meetings of organizations I belong to feeling somewhat tied in, rather than isolated, out of place, outnumbered, unheard, held at a distance, or feared.

28. I can be pretty sure that an argument with a colleague of another race is more likely to jeopardize her chances for advancement than to jeopardize mine.

29. I can be fairly sure that if I argue for the promotion of a person of another race, or a program centering on race, this is not likely to cost me heavily within my present setting, even if my colleagues disagree with me.

30. If I declare there is a racial issue at hand, or there isn't a racial issue at hand, my race will lend me more credibility for either position than a person of color will have.

31. I can choose to ignore developments in minority writing and minority activist programs, or disparage them, or learn from them, but in any case, I can find ways to be more or less protected from negative consequences of any of these choices.

32. My culture gives me little fear about ignoring the perspectives and powers of people of other races.

33. I am not made acutely aware that my shape, bearing, or body odor will be taken as a reflection on my race.

34. I can worry about racism without being seen as self-interested or self-seeking.

35. I can take a job with an affirmative action employer without having my co-workers on the job suspect that I got it because of my race.

36. If my day, week, or year is going badly, I need not ask of each negative episode or situation whether it has racial overtones.

37. I can be pretty sure of finding people who would be willing to talk with me and advise me about my next steps, professionally.

38. I can think over many options, social, political, imaginative, or professional, without asking whether a person of my race would be accepted or allowed to do what I want to do.

39. I can be late to a meeting without having the lateness reflect on my race.
40. I can choose public accommodation without fearing that people of my race cannot get in or will be mistreated in the places I have chosen.
41. I can be sure that if I need legal or medical help, my race will not work against me.
42. I can arrange my activities so that I will never have to experience feelings of rejection owing to my race.
43. If I have low credibility as a leader, I can be sure that my race is not the problem.
44. I can easily find academic courses and institutions that give attention only to people of my race.
45. I can expect figurative language and imagery in all of the arts to testify to experiences of my race.
46. I can choose blemish cover or bandages in "flesh" color and have them more or less match my skin.

Count up the number of "yes" responses and "no" responses. How many did you have? Are you surprised by the numbers?

Which items received a "no" response? Why? Was your "no" because of your race, or was it because of something else?

Now take out a piece of paper. Spend 15 minutes free-writing about this exercise. Are there privileges that you have that you weren't aware of? What about privileges that have been denied to you—were any of these surprising? How did this exercise make you feel?

Q IS FOR

QUEER

I took Human Sexuality when I was in college (which, by the way, was far more informative than the sex education experiences I had in high school). The day we were scheduled to focus on "Homosexuality" (that's what the lecture topic was called in the syllabus), the professor had invited a panel of gay men and lesbian women to share their experiences and facilitate a class discussion. It was an interesting class session, and I learned a lot. But one of the panelists, a lesbian woman, said something that really stuck with me:

> *"I wake up in the morning, go to work, and come home to my partner. We spend quality time together, and we also argue about dumb things, like whose turn it is to do the dishes. I pay taxes, walk the dog, and take out the garbage. I'm just like everyone else."*

That's a good thing, right? To be just like everyone else? For a lot of people in historically marginalized communities, that's exactly what they want. But for some people, they don't want to fit in, or be "the same." They want to be themselves—to express their own unique, quirky, offbeat, culturally different, gender-bending, don't-fit-neatly-into-a-box identities. They are *queer*, and squeezing themselves into an identity box involves a huge amount of sacrifice for them.

Let's back up a little bit. Many people use the term *queer* to refer specifically to the lesbian, gay, bisexual, and transgender (LGBT) community—and quite a few people use the terms queer and LGBT interchangeably. But increasingly, people are making a distinction between the two terms. For many people, LGBT is a sexual or gender identity. Queer, in contrast, is a political identity.

What does that mean, exactly? Some people in the LGBT community embrace their identities, but don't want to be politically involved. They want to get a good job, get married, have kids, and live a comfortable life—all of the things that are *heteronormative* (valued and privileged by heterosexual society). They want to be "just like everyone else." They're engaging in what some people refer to as *homonormativity*, which involves being out and open about one's identity, yet creating a way of living that mimics heterosexuality in order to gain acceptance. Essentially, they're engaging in *respectability politics*, by demonstrating that their behaviors are compatible with mainstream values.

Historically, people in marginalized communities have felt pressured to engage in respectability politics. Act White. Be straight-acting. If you're transgender, do everything you can to "pass"—meaning, look cisgender. Assimilate. Blend in. Play nice. (That's a common one for activists.) Don't stand out. Don't cause trouble.

But that's not what everyone wants, and it's not always the best way to effect change. That's where the word "queer" comes in. But what does it mean to identify as queer?

- Queer can be an umbrella term used synonymously with LGBT, referring to people who are marginalized because of their sexual or gender identities.
- Queer can refer to people who don't fit into traditional norms of sexuality and gender identity/expression, and their preferred

relationships may be nontraditional (such as non-monogamous relationships).

- Queer can be a label used by people who experience attractions in a non-binary way. They might be attracted to males, females, or people who are genderqueer or otherwise gender non-conforming. Or their attractions might have nothing to do with gender—some people who experience this refer to themselves as *pansexual.*
- Queer can be a sign of being revolutionary, transgressive, and anti-assimilation. They challenge the status quo and celebrate being different.
- For many people, especially for those who are older, queer can be a slur used against someone who is perceived to be gay or lesbian. Some people are very uncomfortable with reclaiming and using the word "queer," because they can recall vividly how it felt when that word was used against them.

There's a lot of overlap between queer politics and feminism. A good definition of "queer feminism" is this one, from http://queer feminism.com:

A radical opposition to patriarchy, a system that includes:

- *Racism, imperialism, genocide, and violence;*
- *Strict rules about gender and sexuality that hurt everyone, whether male, female, both, or neither;*
- *Blaming and shaming of trans people, queer people, prudes, sluts, and anyone who does not fit a narrow and arbitrary body standard;*
- *Rape culture; and*
- *A tendency to claim that democracy and liberal politics fixes all ills, rather than addressing society's problems.*

Queer feminists (and queer activists in general) commonly engage in grassroots, community-based, guerrilla activism. Their actions create spaces for trans voices, intersex voices, bi voices, non-binary voices, people of color voices, interlocking voices, and in-between voices. "We're here! We're queer! Get used to it!" The classic chant, created by the activist organization Queer Nation, embodies the value of being different and not having to apologize for it. It's the difference between coloring your life within the lines or living outside of them.

FEMINIST HERSTORY: MARSHA JOHNSON AND SYLVIA RIVERA

On June 28, 1969, police raided the Stonewall Inn, a Mafia-owned bar in New York City that was an underground gay hangout. Back then, having an LGBT identity wasn't anywhere near as accepted as it is today, and police raids on gay bars were common. Usually, during a raid, someone would give the patrons of the bar a heads-up so they could run out the back door and get away. This time, though, they didn't run—instead, they resisted and fought back, leading to several days of riots and demonstrations. Many of the participants were those who existed on the fringes of the community, including homeless street kids and transgender people who hung out in Christopher Street Park.

The police raid and subsequent riots went down in history, launching the modern-day LGBT rights movement. However, the contributions of Marsha Johnson and Sylvia Rivera, both transgender women of color, didn't make it into most of the history books. Because their stories have been largely ignored, the Stonewall riots became a symbol of a largely White male movement that kept women, people of color, and transgender people on the margins.

Born Malcolm Michaels, Jr., Marsha Johnson spent her childhood in New Jersey, where she repeatedly was the victim of bigotry and intolerance. She moved to the West Village in New York City in 1966 when she was 22 years old. For the next thirty years, Johnson supported herself by waitressing, panhandling, and engaging in street prostitution. Even though she herself lived in the margins of society, she took on the role of "drag mother" to transgender people and to the queer kids who lived on the streets. She suffered from mental illness and sometimes had uncontrollable bouts of anger, but was mostly known for her generosity towards those who were marginalized.

On June 27, 1969, Johnson went to the Stonewall Inn to celebrate her 25th birthday, and was inside the bar when the police raids started. Most of the patrons made it outside, then barricaded the police inside the Stonewall. It was then that a witness saw Johnson drop a heavy weight onto a police car, one of many acts of resistance that took place over the next few days.

A year after the Stonewall Riots, Johnson and Sylvia Rivera co-founded an organization called STAR (Street Transvestite Action Revolutionaries), which had a strong presence at gay liberation marches and other radical political venues. An offshoot of that organization was STAR House, which provided services to homeless transgender youth. During the 1980s, Johnson became involved with the AIDS Coalition to Unleash Power (ACT-UP), engaging in demonstrations, marches, sit-ins, and various forms of political theater. She performed in Andy Warhol's drag queen performance troupe, Hot Peaches, and was a subject of one of Warhol's photo shoots.

Throughout her life, Johnson had been arrested numerous times (she claimed over one hundred), suffered from at least eight serious psychiatric episodes, and experienced several attempts on her life by "johns." In 1992, shortly after the New York Pride March, Johnson's body was found floating in the Hudson River. She was 48 when she died, and her case remains unsolved.

Sylvia Rivera was one of Marsha Johnson's mentees. Born in New York as Ray Rivera Mendosa, Rivera lived a turbulent childhood. When she was three, her stepfather threatened to kill her and her mother, and shortly afterwards her mother committed suicide. Even as a young child, Rivera refused to conform to masculine gender expectations; by the 4th grade, Rivera refused to hide in the closet and was wearing makeup to school. Back then, anyone who engaged in gender nonconforming behavior was severely penalized, which was the case for Rivera. By the time she was ten, she had left home and was living on the streets of Times Square working as a street prostitute. Life on the streets was very dangerous; drugs and violence were ever-present, and she was sexually assaulted while working the streets. Moreover, Rivera couldn't count on the police to keep her safe; in fact, Rivera once jumped out of a moving police car in order to resist arrest.

Rivera was seventeen years old when the Stonewall Riots took place. When the police raid started, she was part of the crowd that gathered outside the bar. "I'm not missing a minute of this," she yelled. "It's the revolution!" As police began escorting people from the bar, Rivera was one of the first protestors to throw a bottle—an action that shifted the dynamic from "raid" to "riot."

In addition to co-founding STAR with Marsha Johnson, Rivera joined the Gay Activists Alliance (GAA) and participated in numerous political actions. In a campaign to pass the New York City Gay Rights Bill, Rivera famously crashed a meeting at City Hall by climbing the walls in a dress and high heels. Later, in an effort to appeal to a broader population, the GAA removed "drag" and "transvestite" issues from their political agenda, and Rivera became increasingly disillusioned by the racism and transphobia in the gay community. She was famously quoted in an interview as saying, "Hell hath no fury like a drag queen scorned."

Sylvia Rivera died of liver cancer at the age of 50. Her legacy lives on through an organization called the Sylvia Rivera Law Project (SRLP), which works to end poverty and transgender discrimination. In 2005, a street near the Stonewall Inn was named after Rivera.

TRY THIS!

It can be very challenging for transgender youth to be out and open about their identities. This exercise is designed to raise awareness about those challenges. If you are transgender, think about whether you feel very safe, unsure, or very unsafe in each of these scenarios, then circle the appropriate response. If you are not transgender, imagine what it might be like for someone who is, then respond to each item.

In class

Very safe   Unsure   Very unsafe

On your school's campus

Very safe   Unsure   Very unsafe

In the cafeteria

Very safe   Unsure   Very unsafe

At gym class

Very safe   Unsure   Very unsafe

In the restroom

Very safe   Unsure   Very unsafe

At an afterschool club

Very safe   Unsure   Very unsafe

At your school's Gay-Straight Alliance (GSA)

Very safe   Unsure   Very unsafe

On a school overnight trip

Very safe   Unsure   Very unsafe

At a movie theater

Very safe   Unsure   Very unsafe

At a Pride parade

Very safe   Unsure   Very unsafe

At a local LGBT center

Very safe   Unsure   Very unsafe

At a school football game

Very safe   Unsure   Very unsafe

At a restaurant

Very safe   Unsure   Very unsafe

At a family event

Very safe   Unsure   Very unsafe

At work

Very safe   Unsure   Very unsafe

Hanging out with friends

Very safe   Unsure   Very unsafe

At the beach

Very safe   Unsure   Very unsafe

At the doctor's office

Very safe   Unsure   Very unsafe

Now, answer these questions:

- How did it feel to reflect on each of these situations?
- How might these opinions be different for a transgender person, compared to a lesbian, gay, or bisexual person? Can transphobia exist in gay and lesbian communities, or are those safe spaces for most transgender people?
- Do race and ethnicity make a difference? Would your responses be different for transgender people of color?
- Does gender make a difference? Would your responses be different for transgirls vs. transboys? What about for people whose gender is nonbinary?
- Does being queer make a difference? How do these scenarios play out for people who embrace queer politics?
- What have you learned as a result of doing this exercise?

You can also do this activity in a large group. It's really powerful if you create a giant, room-size rating scale, where one end is labeled "Very Safe," the middle is labeled "Unsure," and the opposite end is labeled "Very Unsafe." Ask participants to imagine how safe they think it is for transgender youth to be "out" in each of these situations. Then ask them to stand in the part of the room that best reflects their opinion. Afterwards, hold a group discussion, referring to the questions listed above.

IS FOR

ASK ABOUT LESBIAN LIVES

RADICAL

Ask your friends if they believe men and women should have equal rights and opportunities. I bet they'll say:

"Yes!"
"Totally!"
"Of course!"

Then ask them if they use the term "feminist" to identify themselves. I bet you'll get responses like these:

"No, that's too strong of a word."
"I wouldn't go that far."
"I'm not that radical."

Tally up your responses. Now compare them to these findings: According to one poll, 82% of participants said that "men and women should be social, political, and economic equals." But only 20% of those same participants considered themselves to be feminists. Interesting, huh? And that's not all—many celebrities say exactly the same thing:

"No, I wouldn't say feminist—that's too strong."
—Kelly Clarkson

"I'm not a feminist. I hail men, I love men, I celebrate American male culture—beer, bars, and muscle cars."
—Lady Gaga

"I am not a feminist, but I do believe in the strength of women."
—Katy Perry

"I wouldn't go so far as to say I am a feminist, that can come off as a negative connotation. But I am a strong female."
—Carrie Underwood

So most people embrace feminist values, but they're not willing to label themselves with the term. What's that about?

Maybe it's because the word "feminist" conjures up so many negative stereotypes. *Feminists hate men, feminists are ugly, feminists burn bras, feminists are always angry.* All of these perceptions are untrue. The reality is that there are lots of different kinds of feminists. From reading earlier entries in this book, you're already familiar with *liberal feminists*, who focus on achieving equal rights in the workplace, education, and politics. *Marxist* and *socialist feminists* believe that capitalism is a direct cause of gender inequality. *Cultural feminists* believe that women are fundamentally different from men, and that feminine qualities (such as intuition and emotional connectedness) should be valued and celebrated. *Women of color femi-*

148

nists focus on how racism intersects with sexism. *Ecofeminists* make connections between the oppression of women and mistreating our natural environment. *Transfeminists* advocate for the liberation of all women, including transgender women. And the goal of *radical feminists* is to dismantle the patriarchy—a male-dominated power structure woven throughout society.

That's just the tip of the iceberg—there are many more feminist philosophies out there. At least one of them will likely resonate with you. Still, the word "feminism" causes many people to recoil, as if it might bite them if they got too close.

Amazing, really. How can one, eight-letter word hold so much power? Maybe that's why so many people shy away from it—because it has the power to create radical change. Imagine how different the world would be if we claimed the power of feminism, rather than running away from it.

> *"I am basically a feminist. I think that women can do anything they decide to do."*
> —Grace Kelly

> *"For everyone, men and women, it's important to be a feminist."*
> —Mindy Kaling

> *"I am a modern-day feminist."*
> —Beyoncé

FEMINIST HERSTORY: THE LESBIAN AVENGERS

It was 1992. Millions of people worldwide had died from AIDS, and the deaths were continuing with no effective treatment in sight. Abortion rights for women were being chipped away, and anti-abortion groups were gaining political traction. That year, activists participated in marches and political demonstrations to make AIDS a policy issue in the upcoming presidential election. They marched on Washington in support of abortion rights and lesbian women were right at the forefront of both of those efforts.

But over time, lesbians were getting tired of focusing their energies on AIDS and abortion when no one was devoting any attention to their own issues. They became increasingly frustrated with invisibility and marginalization in society, and with sexism and misogyny within the gay community. So they took action and formed a group called the Lesbian Avengers, a direct action group focused on issues vital to lesbian survival and visibility.

The Lesbian Avengers was founded by six lesbian activists, all of whom were involved in a variety of LGBT groups. They met over dinner, came up with a name, hammered out a political strategy, and created a flyer to distribute at the New York Gay Pride. "LESBIANS! DYKES! GAY WOMEN!" it said. "We're wasting our lives being careful. Imagine what your life could be. Aren't you ready to make it happen?" Their first meeting drew a large group, and within a couple of months they launched their first direct action—a demonstration in Queens in support of the multicultural-themed "Children of the Rainbow" curriculum, which was being challenged because of its inclusion of LGBT people. Lesbians who participated in the action handed out balloons to children and parents that said "Ask about lesbian lives," while wearing T-shirts that read, "I was a lesbian child." A few months later, the Lesbian Avengers went to the home of Mary Cummins, an outspoken opponent of the Rainbow curriculum, and publicly serenaded her. These were the kinds of actions the Lesbian Avengers took; instead of engaging in traditional actions like circulating a petition or organizing a sit-in, they encouraged actions that were edgy, dramatic, rebellious, and theatrical.

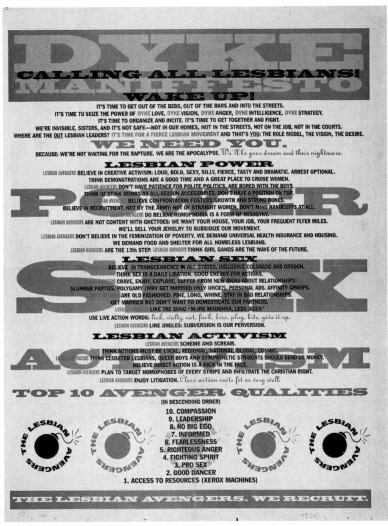

"It's time for DYKE love, DYKE vision, DYKE anger, DYKE intelligence, DYKE strategy." The Lesbian Avenger Dyke Manifesto was a call to action, inspiring those on the sidelines of the gay rights movement and the feminist movement to come together and launch a "fierce lesbian movement." If you had read this poster in 1992 when the group formed, would you have been inspired to join? Why or why not? *Credit:* Lesbian Avengers and Carrie Moyer (designer)

Lesbian Avenger chapters sprung up all over the world. In Colorado, they chained themselves to the gate of the Governor's Mansion as a protest against Amendment 2, which prohibited towns, cities, and counties in the state from recognizing lesbian, gay, and bisexual people as a protected class. In Austin, Texas, a group of Avengers protested sodomy laws by invading the State Capitol and hoisting banners, flying paper airplanes, and launching stink bombs. And in San Francisco, Avengers unleashed a swarm of locusts onto the headquarters of Exodus International, a religious-based group that endorsed therapy to change one's sexual orientation.

Fire-eating became the Lesbian Avengers trademark action. Their first fire-eating action was in response to the deaths of a lesbian and gay man, who were burned to death after a Molotov cocktail was thrown into their apartment. A month later, the Avengers staged an action where they ate fire, chanting "The fire will not consume us. We take it and make it our own."

In 1993, the night before the March on Washington for Lesbian, Gay, and Bisexual Rights, the Lesbian Avengers organized the first Dyke March. Twenty thousand women took to the streets, and a dozen Lesbian Avengers, using a dramatic form of political theater, ate fire in front of the White House. That June, several cities hosted Dyke Marches in conjunction with their annual LGBT Pride celebrations, and a number of cities still organize Dyke Marches today. San Francisco and New York hold the largest marches, attracting thousands of lesbian, bisexual, trans, and queer-identified women.

TRY THIS!

Are you familiar with conversation starter cards? If not, here's an opportunity for you! At the end of this chapter is a set of "feminism conversation starter" cards. Photocopy or scan and print the page, then

This flyer was handed out at many Lesbian Avenger events and demonstrations. The phrase "we recruit" is a thinly-veiled reference to Anita Bryant, an evangelical Christian who in 1977 formed an organization called "Save Our Children." Her belief was that because gays and lesbians couldn't reproduce, they instead recruited children into homosexuality. *Credit:* Lesbian Avengers and Carrie Moyer (designer)

cut out each of the cards. Use the cards with your family, a group of friends, an afterschool club, or a community organization.

Ask the group to create a set of ground rules for these conversations. You might consider including the following:

- Don't interrupt. Allow each person to finish their thought before speaking.
- Listen to what the person is saying. Don't formulate a counter-argument while they're talking.
- Don't engage in name-calling, insults, or attacks on a person's character.
- Try to see the issue from the other person's perspective before saying what you think.
- If someone says something that you don't understand, ask for clarification.
- Be willing to be uncomfortable. Discomfort is where growth and learning happen.

What does the word "feminism" mean to you?	What got you interested in feminism?	If you could meet any feminist in history, who would it be? What would you want to discuss with this person?
If you could imagine a world without sexism, what would that look like?	What do you think is the most important feminist issue today? Why?	Which feminist philosophy resonates with you the most? Why?
Why do you think so many people refuse to identify as feminists?	Can boys and men be feminists? If so, how can they be included in the feminist movement?	Do you think that feminism has been inclusive of everyone, or not? If not, what groups or issues have been excluded?
If a woman marries a man, is it "feminist" if she takes his last name? What if she marries a woman—in that situation, is taking her spouse's last name okay?	What form of oppression impacts you the most? Why?	Are there forms of feminist activism that you think are inappropriate? Why?
What's your opinion about abortion? Should it be legal, or not? Should there be any restrictions on abortion?	Does the U.S. Constitution need an Equal Rights Amendment?	Should reproductive health services be covered by employer or government insurance plans? Why or why not? What about transgender-related health services?

IS FOR

SAME JOB

SUPERGIRL

"You can do anything you set your mind to!"

This is of the most powerful messages girls in the U.S. receive today—and to a large degree, that's true. The opportunities that are available for girls and women stretch way beyond getting married, having children, and days spent cleaning the house and doing laundry. You can be a doctor, a lawyer, an artist, a writer, an educator, a computer programmer, a pilot, or the CEO of a corporation—just to name a few options. In fact, you can pursue any of these careers AND get married, have children, and be a domestic goddess. Right?

Girls and women can do anything. I believe that down to my bones. But that doesn't mean that we can do EVERYTHING—or that we should *have* to do everything. And we certainly don't have to be perfect. Perfection is an illusion. Unfortunately, many girls and women take on way too many responsibilities, and then feel as if they need to handle all of them perfectly and effortlessly. That's the *Supergirl Complex*, and in my opinion, it's incredibly dangerous, for several reasons.

First, let's explore a couple of things that are going on at the psychological level. Sometimes we have difficulty meeting the expectations of others (or of ourselves) because the expectations are unrealistic. Psychologists call this *role strain*. Feeling overwhelmed with academic demands at school is a common example. To complicate things more, most of us have multiple roles and responsibilities in our lives, and sometimes those roles interfere with one another. You may love playing in the school band, but you find it difficult to participate in band, meet your school obligations, and still have time to hang out with your friends. That's called *role conflict*.

Now, let's talk about the social and cultural factors behind the Supergirl Complex—because we know, as feminists, that everything happens within a social, cultural, economic, and political context. Here are a few things to think about:

Women are paid less than men in the workforce, and generally, people of color are paid less than White women. You've probably heard of the "wage gap," or the difference between what men earn and what women earn. As of this writing, the gender wage gap is 79 cents to the dollar—meaning that for every dollar a man earns, a woman, on average, earns 79 cents. When we consider race and ethnicity in conjunction with gender, the picture becomes more complicated. For every dollar a White male earns, a White woman earns 75 cents, an Asian-American woman earns 90 cents, Native Hawaiian and other Pacific Islander women earn 60 cents, American Indian and Alaska native women earn 58 cents, African-American women earn 62 cents, and Latina women earn 54 cents. These are grave disparities. In essence, for a woman to make as much as a man does, she needs to work harder and longer.

Women are expected to work for free. The phrase "women's work" usually refers to unpaid labor in the household, including childcare, housework, cooking, laundry, and other domestic tasks. Some women do this full-time. Other women take on what sociologist Arlie Hochschild calls "the second shift"—the unpaid domestic work they do after they come home from their paid job. When her book, *The Second Shift*, was published in 1989, Hochschild estimated that, on average, women were working an extra month more per year than their male spouses. Almost three decades later, women have made significant strides in the paid workforce, but the amount of "second shift" work they do hasn't changed much.

Girls and women are often expected to perform "emotional labor." Imagine working in a restaurant as a server and your customer is "high-maintenance." She keeps dropping her fork and asking you for a new one. When her order arrives, she's dissatisfied and sends it back to the kitchen. What do you do in this situation? You give her what she wants, and you do it with a smile on your face because your job is to keep the customer happy, while keeping your own feelings in check. That's "emotional labor"—and women who do it (because it's mostly women) don't get paid enough for it.

In a nutshell, women earn less while they're doing more. No wonder women experience role strain and role conflict!

Two feminist theories can give us a framework for this reality. *Marxist feminism*, based on the economic theories of Karl Marx, recognizes that a gendered division of labor exists within a capitalist economic system. Males are more likely to perform *productive labor*, which refers to work that translates into monetary value. Women, on the other hand, engage in what's called *reproductive labor* (also referred to as *unproductive labor*), which involves unpaid household and family caregiving labor. This gendered division of labor, coupled with the wage gap and occupational segregation (the fact that some jobs are dominated by men, and others by women), are the foundation of women's oppression.

Some feminists argue that it's too simplistic to put all the blame on capitalism because sexism and misogyny also exist in non-capitalistic societies. That's where *socialist feminism* comes in, which is a blend between Marxist feminism and radical feminism. First coined by the Chicago Women's Liberation Union in 1972, socialist feminism argues that both patriarchy *and* economic inequality contribute to women's oppression. In order to eliminate gender inequities, all other forms of oppression also need to be addressed, including racism, homophobia and heterosexism, transphobia, and class oppression. You can't get rid of one without addressing all the others.

You can do anything. Truly. All of us have an inner Supergirl, and it's always exciting to see her come out. But remember, when you're feeling tired, or overwhelmed, or not-quite-good-enough, it's not because there's something wrong with you. You don't need fixing—the system does!

FEMINIST HERSTORY: LUCY PARSONS AND THE INDUSTRIAL WORKERS OF THE WORLD

Most high school history and social studies classes cover the labor movement of the early 1900s, which advocated for higher wages, better hours, and improved working conditions. One of the first organized labor unions was the American Federation of Labor, founded by Samuel Gompers. The AFL was an umbrella group of smaller labor unions, most of which represented men who were skilled workers. African-Americans, unskilled laborers, and women were typically excluded from these unions, and there was little support for women's attempts to unionize. In fact, the leadership of the AFL, including Gompers, believed that women were a threat to men's jobs. From that point forward, and even today, union organizing has been heavily male-dominated.

But that didn't stop all women, especially not Lucy Parsons. As is the case with so many historical women, not much information about her has been written down, and the information that is available isn't always consistent. Here's what we do know: She was born as Lucy Gonzalez in 1853, probably into slavery. She was probably born in Texas, but other accounts suggest that she may have been born in Virginia. She was of Mexican-American, African-American, and Native American heritage. When she was emancipated, she met Albert Parsons, a labor organizer and ex-Confederate soldier, and they married in 1871. Their interracial marriage, which was highly taboo at the time, led to direct conflict with the local Ku Klux Klan. Because of that, the couple was forced to leave Texas, and they eventually settled in Chicago, Illinois.

On May 4, 1886, a peaceful rally in support of an eight-hour workday, and in protest of a series of workers who were killed by the police the previous day, was held in Haymarket Square in Chicago. Both Lucy and Albert Parsons attended the rally. At some point during the demonstration, police charged the crowd, and someone threw a stick of dynamite. The police drew fire, and in the end, seven police officers and at least four civilians were killed. This event in history is now known as the "Haymarket Affair" or the "Haymarket Riot." Later, Albert Parsons was one of the protestors who was charged by the police. Lucy led the campaign to exonerate the "Haymarket Martyrs," but her husband was ultimately convicted and hanged.

After her husband's execution, Lucy continued to participate in labor organizing. Among other things, she organized door-to-door campaigns in rich neighborhoods, where poor women knocked on doors and confronted wealthy homeowners. She marched on picket lines, participated in rallies and demonstrations, and openly challenged politicians at public meetings. A member of the Chicago Police Department described her as "more dangerous than a thousand rioters."

On June 24, 1905, a group of over 200 radical labor organizers, one of whom was Lucy Parsons, held a convention to oppose the policies of the American Federation of Labor (AFL). This led to the formation of the Industrial Workers of the World (IWW), a militant group rooted in socialist principles. Lucy was the only woman of color, and one of only two women delegates (the other was Mother Jones) at the founding convention. She was the only woman to give a speech (below), in which she advocated fiercely for the rights of all workers, particularly women.

We, the women of this country, have no ballot even if we wished to use it, and the only way that we can be represented is to take a man to represent us. You men have made such a mess of it in representing us that we have not much confidence in asking you . . .

We [women] are the slaves of slaves. We are exploited more ruthlessly than men. Whenever wages are to be reduced the capitalist class use women to reduce them, and if there is anything that you men should do in the future it is to organize the women . . .

Now, what do we mean when we say revolutionary Socialist?

We mean that the land shall belong to the landless, the tools to the toiler, and the products to the producers . . . I believe that if every man and every woman who works, or who toils in the mines, mills, the workshops, the fields, the factories and the farms of our broad America should decide in their minds that they shall have that which of right belongs to them, and that no idler shall live upon their toil . . . then there is no army that is large enough to overcome you, for you yourselves constitute the army . . .

My conception of the strike of the future is not to strike and go out and starve, but to strike and remain in and take possession of the necessary property of production . . .

. . . Let us sink such differences as nationality, religion, politics, and set our eyes eternally and forever toward the rising star of the industrial republic of labor; remembering that we have left the old behind and have set our faces toward the future. There is no power on earth that can stop men and women who are determined to be free at all hazards. There is no power on earth so great as the power of intellect. It moves the world and it moves the earth . . .

I hope even now to live to see the day when the first dawn of the new era of labor will have arisen, when capitalism will be a thing of the past, and the new industrial republic, the commonwealth of labor, shall be in operation.
I thank you.

While Lucy Parsons is best known for her labor organizing efforts, she was also an active feminist, believing that women's oppression stemmed from capitalism. She also advocated for the rights of people of color, as well as for political prisoners. Many historians believe that Lucy Parsons helped lay the groundwork for the sit-down strikes in Detroit in the 1930s, the Civil Rights movement of the 1950s and 1960s, and the Occupy Wall Street movement that began in 2011.

Parsons died in 1952, when a fire raged through her home in Chicago. She was 89 years old. By the time friends arrived at her home, FBI agents and members of the Chicago Police Department had seized her collection of books, manuscripts, papers, and other documents. They have never been returned.

TRY THIS!

Think about how you've earned money in your life. Did you get an allowance? Did you babysit? Have you had a summer job, or an afterschool job? If the answer to any of these questions is "yes," did you accept without question what your employer (or your family, in the case of an allowance) said they would pay you? Did you try to negotiate a higher wage? If you didn't, don't beat up on yourself; the reality is that, while males frequently negotiate better salaries, females may not always think to do that. The next time you accept a job offer, try these tactics for increasing your pay. Even if you have little to no experience, and you're offered minimum wage, chances are good that if you negotiate, you'll end up with more money.

Step 1: Research

- Do your research. What's the going rate for jobs like yours? Go online and find out what typical pay rates are for specific jobs. If you have friends who work in similar jobs, you could ask them what they make. But be careful, and proceed with caution. Some people find questions about money to be intrusive. In addition, if your friend didn't negotiate for a higher wage, asking questions about this issue could cause resentment.
- Establish a realistic goal. If you babysit, and the going rate in your area is $15/hour, start with that as a baseline. Consider factors like: will you be responsible for multiple children? How old are they? Will you be expected to care for infants? All of these factors could influence your pay rate—if you ask.

Step 2: Planning

- Think about what you want to say. If you're nervous about asking for more money, practice with a friend beforehand, and ask your friend to give you feedback.
- Start with the low-hanging fruit. If, for example, your employer is offering you $9.75/hour, see if they'd be willing to bump it up to $10.00. That might not seem like much, but the extra twenty-five cents will make a big difference over time. If you're a babysitter and your employer expects you to pick up the children from school, ask if you can be reimbursed for mileage. These are simple requests, and employers are likely to say "yes."
- Focus on the positive. Don't downplay your skills. Remember, this employer hired you because they thought you'd be good at the job! Highlight the skills that you bring to the position.

Step 3: Reflection

- Listen to your employer. They might say "no" to your request, but with the caveat that they'll consider a pay increase in six months, depending on your job performance.
- When your employer makes an offer, take some time to think about it. Don't accept or reject it on the spot. Ask if you can have 24 hours to mull it over. If your employer wants an answer sooner than that, ask if you can get back to them later that day.
- Whatever the outcome, thank your employer for considering your request. A little appreciation goes a long way.
- Give yourself a big pat on the back. If you were able to negotiate a higher wage, congratulations! And if your employer rejected your request, pat yourself on the back anyway. For many girls and women, asking for higher pay is *really* hard—but you did it anyway! That's something to celebrate.

T IS FOR

FEMINIST

FEAR

TOUGH

"Come on, boy! Man up! Stop that crying!"

I overheard a man say this after his young son fell off a swing at the playground. After he said this, the little boy started sniffling, and it looked like he was using every ounce of energy to hold back those tears. It was painful to watch. Immediately, two thoughts went through my mind.

Thought #1: *Already he's getting the message that "boys don't cry."*

Thought #2: *He's probably, what, four? And his dad is telling him to "man up"?*

No matter your gender, humans are hard-wired to experience six different emotions—anger, joy, surprise, disgust, fear, and sadness. No matter what country or culture they're from, people are born with the capacity to feel and express all of these. But the last two—fear and sadness—are considered to be less "manly."

When girls are afraid, we try to protect and soothe them.

When boys are afraid, we tell them to toughen up and be brave.

When girls cry, we comfort them.

When boys cry, we tell them to stop.

Jackson Katz, a media educator and former football player, asked young men what it means to be a man in our culture. The responses he got included the following:

- Strong
- Physical
- Independent
- In control
- Powerful
- Athletic
- Tough

Get tough. Grow a pair. Man up. These are the messages that boys get. And then they have to demonstrate, again and again and again, that they're worthy of hanging on to their "man card." This can be particularly true in communities of color. In a culture that marginalizes people because of their race, ethnicity, or culture, there's a much stronger incentive for boys and men of color to grasp more tightly to their male privilege.

All of this isn't without serious repercussions—forcing yourself to suppress your feelings over time can have a serious impact on your physical and mental health. Interestingly, while media portrayals of women have gotten thinner over the years, males in the media have become stronger and more aggressive over time. And according to FBI statistics, the vast majority of violent crimes are committed by men. Let's use a specific example to explore these concepts further.

Thursday, December 13, 2012. It was the last day of my Psychology of Women class. The topic of the day was "Men and Masculinity," and the movie of the day was a documentary called *Tough Guise*. Narrated by Jackson Katz and directed by Sut Jhally, *Tough Guise* links the increase of male violence, misogyny, and homophobia to the way we define manhood and masculinity in American culture. Over the course of the film, Katz examines violence in professional sports, sexualized violence in the media, homophobia-driven violence towards men who violate gender norms, and the role of masculinity in school shootings, including the tragedies in Littleton, Colorado and Jonesboro, Arkansas. It's a powerful film, never failing to spark thoughtful discussion among my students.

Friday, December 14, 2012. I got to my office, turned on the computer, and scanned the headlines of my regular go-to online publications. And what was the first headline I saw?

SHOOTING REPORTED AT CONNECTICUT ELEMENTARY SCHOOL

Twenty-seven deaths—twenty of them children. How on earth do you wrap your head around something like this? My first reaction was disbelief, followed by an intense desire to protect my own child. And the fact that just the day before I had shown a film that, in part, examined the reasons behind school shootings felt more than a little chilling.

Here's what else was unnerving. After the shootings at Columbine High School in 1999, the *New York Times* published a number of front-page articles that attempted to unpack the reasons why Eric Harris and Dylan Klebold would open gunfire on their classmates and teachers. Among the reasons cited included the usual suspects: video game violence, social ostracism, lack of mental health prevention and services, overly permissive gun laws. And yet, as Jackson Katz pointed out in the film, one obvious factor was completely overlooked. "It's not just 'kids killing kids,'" says Katz, "It's *boys* who are shooting boys, and *boys* who are shooting girls." Naming the obvious—the fact that boys are almost always the shooters—opens the door for a discussion about masculinity, power, and violence.

Within hours after the news broke about the shooting at Sandy Hook Elementary, the media began to speculate about the underlying causes of this most recent tragedy. Guess what they focused on? *Gun control. Mental health. Media violence. School security.* And yet again, the fact that a *man* was the shooter wasn't even a part of the discussion.

I want to make it very clear that I'm not trying to be a male-basher. The vast majority of men do not engage in violence. However, it's important to note that the men who do engage in violence are responsible for most of the violent crimes in the United States. Check out these facts:

- Over 85% of people who commit murder are men (and the women who commit murder often do so as a defense against their male batterers);
- In 90% of homicides, both the victim and the perpetrator are men;
- Men commit 95% of serious domestic violence;
- 99.8% of those in prison convicted of rape are men;
- 84% of hate crime perpetrators are men.

These statistics are staggering. And yet, it's important to clarify that merely being a man isn't the primary factor associated with violence. The "X" factor, according to the research, is *masculinity* in men—and the threat of losing it. For many men, getting your "man card" taken away is the worst possible thing that could ever happen to you, and some men will do whatever it takes to salvage whatever shred of their "man card" they can hold onto. According to sociologists Rachel Kalish and Michael Kimmel, this is exactly what motivates boys to engage in school shootings:

*These perpetrators were not just misguided 'kids', or 'youth'
or 'troubled teens'—they're boys. They are a group of boys,
deeply aggrieved by a system that they may feel is cruel or
demeaning. . . . What transforms the aggrieved into mass mur-
ders is also a sense of entitlement, a sense of using violence
against others, making others hurt as you, yourself, might hurt.
Aggrieved entitlement inspires revenge against those who have
wronged you; it is the compensation for humiliation. Humiliation is emasculation: humiliate someone and you take away
his manhood. For many men, humiliation must be avenged, or
you cease to be a man.*

"Aggrieved entitlement"—now there's a whole different lens
through which to consider violent crimes. Numerous studies indicate that, among men who perpetrate violence, masculine identity
(or the threat of losing it) is a primary motivating factor behind
rape, sexual assault, intimate partner violence, and hate crimes, particularly those crimes targeting the LGBTQ community. It makes
perfect sense, if you think about it. Expressing violence towards the
feminine (or, more appropriately, the "not-masculine"), is a powerful way of reinforcing one's manhood. No wonder women are far
more likely than men to be victims of rape. No wonder the highest
rates of LGBTQ-related hate crimes are perpetrated against gay men
and transwomen—two groups that fly in the face of a traditional
masculine identity.

What if a new definition of manhood didn't center around
strength, power, and violence, but rather on having the courage to
show love, compassion, fear, sadness, vulnerability? What if we considered a "real man" to be someone who has the courage to stand
up for the rights of all people, and who won't tolerate any form of
oppression, discrimination, or violence?

FEMINIST HERSTORY: MEN AND FEMINISM

Can a man be a feminist? Those who answer "no" might say, "Men can't understand what it's like to be a woman." Or they might say, "If men can be feminists, then they might take charge of the feminist movement. And then they'd be in charge, which is what feminists are fighting against."

Both are good points. But what about those who answer "yes" to that question? They might say, "There's power in numbers. If men call themselves feminists and join the feminist movement, then there are more people fighting against the patriarchy." Some might say, "Of course men can be feminists. Men stand to benefit from feminism just as much as women." And some make this point: "When a man calls himself a feminist, that in and of itself is a powerful act. Because most men would NEVER call themselves a feminist."

Sadly, there's a lot of truth in that last statement. Because very few men in history have fought to advocate for women's rights—but some have.

Let's start with Frederick Douglass, the famous abolitionist. He was one of just a few men to attend the 1848 Seneca Falls convention, the event that sparked the women's suffrage movement. In 1888, Douglass made a speech that clearly and unequivocally showed his understanding of the power of women's voices:

Woman knows and feels her wrongs as man cannot know and feel them, and she also knows as well as he can know, what measures are needed to redress them. I grant all the claims at this point. She is her own best representative. We can neither speak for her, nor vote for her, nor act for her, nor be responsible for her; and the thing for men to do in the premises is just to get out of her way and give her the fullest opportunity to exercise all the powers inherent in her individual personality, and allow her to do it as she herself shall elect to exercise them.

Then there's John Stuart Mill, who in 1861 wrote an essay with his wife, Harriet Taylor Mill, called "The Subjection of Women." This essay challenged the biological theories and religious texts used to support the idea that women needed men to take care of them (a common belief back then). The Mills also argued that, for many reasons, women should have the right to vote. John Stuart Mill was someone who walked his talk; not only did he put that idea in writing, but he was also the first member of the British Parliament to introduce a bill granting women the right to vote. In 1886, just a few years after Mill wrote his essay, a minister and abolitionist named Parker Pillsbury co-founded, with Elizabeth Cady Stanton, a radical women's rights publication called *Revolution*. He was a vocal advocate for women's suffrage, and because he was a man, he was frequently mocked for it. Name-calling, for example, was common: a typical example was "Granny Pillsbury." Nevertheless, he continued to support and advocate for women's right to vote.

Back then, most men did not support the idea of women's suffrage. But the few that did, particularly the ones who were willing to be vocal about it, helped push the movement forward. And we can see the same thing happening today. There's the National Organization for Men Against Sexism (NOMAS), an organization founded by men that is grounded in four tenets: pro-feminist, gay/LGBT-affirmative, anti-racist, and enhancing men's lives. There's the White Ribbon Campaign, which is a movement of men and boys working to end male violence against women and girls. There's The Good Men Project, a website that provides a forum for a cultural conversation about redefining masculinity, particularly from a feminist perspective. There's Walk a Mile in Her Shoes, which requires men to march in women's heels to raise awareness about sexism and gendered violence. And there are numerous colleges and universities that offer courses in Men and Masculinity Studies, allowing students to explore how patriarchy and rigid sex roles have impacted men—often in a negative way.

So, back to the original question. *Can* men be feminists?

TRY THIS!

Boys don't cry. Or do they? George Washington cried when he took the presidential oath of office. Abraham Lincoln, who often cried in public, did so most famously when Stephen A. Douglas died. Douglas had been his longtime rival and his opponent in the famous Lincoln-Douglas debates. More recently, Barack Obama cried during a speech he gave in the aftermath of the Sandy Hook Elementary School shooting. Clearly, boys and men *do* cry—and we deeply respect them for it.

Let's find out about other famous men who have cried in public. For this activity, you'll need:

- A computer or smart phone with Internet access
- A notebook
- A pen

Take a piece of paper and divide it into two columns. At the top of the left column, write "Men who cried." At the top of the right column, write "Why they cried." You'll come back to this later.

Log on to your computer (or make sure your phone has a good Internet connection). Choose your favorite search engine (such as Google), and type in "famous men who cried in public." When you get your search results, read through several of the articles, and in the left-hand column of your notebook, write down the names of the men who cried. Next to their names, in the right-hand column, write down why they cried.

How many names are on your list? Did some of the names surprise you?

Now, look at the reasons they cried. How "masculine" are these reasons, in your opinion? Are there instances where crying made that person seem weak? If so, why?

Now, let's flip that question around. Were there instances where crying made that person seem strong? If so, why?

U

IS FOR

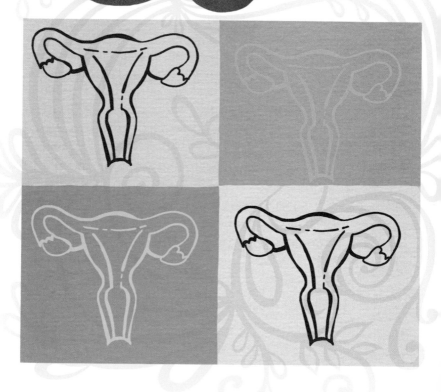

UTERUS

The human body is an amazing and beautiful thing. Regardless of our gender identity, our bodies allow us to do so many things. But if we had to identify the human body part that has endured the most violent attacks and political scrutiny, the uterus quickly rises to the top of the list. Let's look at a few examples.

The abortion controversy is a good place to start, because the uterus is the site of ongoing political debates regarding abortion and the right to choose. If you've ever seen bumper stickers, buttons, or posters with slogans like "Keep your politics out of my uterus!" or "My uterus is my business," you have a sense of just how intensely political abortion, reproductive rights, and freedom of choice are for women. Ever since the landmark *Roe v. Wade* Supreme Court decision in 1973, women have been fighting hard to preserve the right to have an abortion if they choose. And in many states in the U.S., many of those rights have been taken away, making it very difficult for women to fully exercise their freedom of choice.

Then there's the matter of surgeries. Of all of our body parts, the uterus is the one that's the most medicalized; Cesarean sections and hysterectomies occupy the top two slots in the list of most commonly performed surgeries in the U.S. In some cases, these surgeries are completely unnecessary. In other cases, the need for the surgery was provoked by a series of previous medical interventions. Childbirth activists refer to this phenomenon as the "cascade of interventions"—the chain-reaction of unnecessary medical procedures performed on laboring women that inadvertently results in the need for a Cesarean section.

Both of these are critical feminist issues, and both of them involve freedom of choice in some way. In fact, the abortion debate was what galvanized many women in the 1970s to join the second-wave feminist movement. More recently, the childbirth movement has gained significant traction among modern feminists who want to ensure that women are fully informed about their childbirth options and that their choices are honored. Underneath both of those issues, though, is the question of whether or not a person needs to have a uterus in order to be a "real" woman. And that question has caused a deep divide within the feminist community.

Outside of feminist spaces, transmisogyny isn't surprising at all. It happens all the time. In 2012, lots of people boycotted Girl Scout cookies because a Colorado Girl Scout troop allowed a 7-year-old transgender girl to join. Later that year, Jenna Talackova was disqualified from the Miss Universe Canada pageant because she was transgender. And in 2016, North Carolina passed a law, House Bill 2 (HB2), which prevented transgender females from using women's restrooms. All of these examples reflect the idea that, in order to be a "real girl" or a "real woman," you have to have a uterus.

Unfortunately, these kinds of situations have played out in feminist spaces too. One of the clearest examples involves the former Michigan Womyn's Music Festival, an event that was launched in 1976 to provide safe spaces for women, particularly lesbians, to express themselves politically, socially, and creatively. Emerging during the second wave of feminism in the 1970s, women-only spaces were intended as "safe zones" where women could experience freedom from the patriarchal dictates of femininity and womanhood. In women-only spaces (theoretically, at least), a woman is free from the objectification of the "male gaze." She won't have to worry about her voice being ignored, trampled on, and silenced. She won't have to appropriate a masculine persona in order to be heard. And she'll have the freedom to be who she is on her own terms, rather than defining herself in relation to men. Even the term "womyn" was used intentionally as a way to indicate that one doesn't need "man" in order to be "womyn."

It sounds wonderful, right? For many women who identified as feminist, it was. But the darker side of "MichFest" was their womyn-born-womyn policy, which effectively excluded transwomen from this space. In fact, for many years volunteers at MichFest conducted "panty checks" to make sure transgender women weren't trying to sneak in. This perspective is the hallmark of *gender critical feminism*, also referred to by some as *trans-exclusionary radical feminism* (TERF). From their standpoint, not every woman is a "womyn." Inside every transwo*man* is a *man*, like a wolf in sheep's clothing. Cisgender women were born female, raised as girls, and socialized under the dictates of patriarchy. Transwomen were born male and raised as boys, experiencing male privilege along the way. That alone, argue advocates of women-only spaces, makes transwomen not-women.

Both transgender and intersex activists have risen up and fought back against this ideology. ("Intersex" is a general term used to refer to conditions in which a person is born with a sexual or reproductive anatomy that doesn't fit into the standard definition of "male" and "female." It's more common than you might think—some estimate as many as 1 in 200 live births worldwide involve some form of intersex.) In 2001, Emi Koyama published "The Transfeminist Manifesto," launching a new, trans-inclusive form of feminism. Here's an excerpt from the manifesto:

> *Transfeminism is primarily a movement by and for trans women who view their liberation to be intrinsically linked to the liberation of all women and beyond. It is also open to other queers, intersex people, trans men, non-trans women, non-trans men and others who are sympathetic toward needs of trans women and consider their alliance with trans women to be essential for their own liberation. Historically, trans men have made greater contribution to feminism than trans women. We believe that it is imperative that more trans women start participating in the feminist movement alongside others for our liberation.*
>
> *Transfeminism is not about taking over existing feminist institutions. Instead, it extends and advances feminism as a whole through our own liberation and coalition work with all others. It stands up for trans and non-trans women alike, and asks non-trans women to stand up for trans women in return. Transfeminism embodies feminist coalition politics in which women from different backgrounds stand up for each other, because if we do not stand for each other, nobody will.*

So take some time and ask yourself these questions. What makes a girl a girl, or a woman a woman? Is it her body? Is it her experiences? Is it how she's been treated by others? And does a woman need to have a common, unified "woman" experience in order to be a woman?

FEMINIST HERSTORY: ABORTION RIGHTS IN THE U.S.

Abortion is one of the most controversial issues in the United States. Some believe that abortion is murder, an unborn fetus has legal rights, and the government needs to restrict abortion to protect those rights. Others believe that abortion is a widespread practice, that girls and women (not the government) should have the right to decide whether or not to have an abortion, and that safe abortion practices should be available to all. Which viewpoint is correct? It's a complicated issue, but most feminists take the pro-choice side of the debate. Let's look at the history of abortion to understand why.

Abortion has been widely practiced since ancient times, in many areas throughout the world. Most attempts to abort a fetus involved intense exercise, herbal preparations, fasting, bloodletting, and other home preparations. The spread of Christianity caused attitudes about abortion to shift to some extent, although abortion remained legal in Europe for centuries. When Europeans came to the Americas, they brought their attitudes about abortion with them, and abortion remained legal in the U.S. and in western Europe until the 1800s. But the tide began to shift, and the first anti-abortion laws in the U.S. appeared in the 1820s.

What fueled these anti-abortion efforts? The Victorian moral codes of the 1800s, which involved strict social expectations and sexual restraint, probably played a role. Women, particularly in the upper class, were expected to dress modestly, with high-necked blouses and long sweeping skirts, repressing any hint of sexuality. The corset, the ultimate symbol of restraint, was in high fashion during the Victorian era. If a woman adhered to a strict code of social rules and respected the norms of Victorian culture, the reasoning was that there was no need for abortions.

On the opposite end of the spectrum, the women's suffrage movement may have agitated the anti-abortion efforts. Women were gaining power and agency in ways they'd never experienced before, and banning abortion was a way of controlling women and keeping them in their childbearing role. After the Civil War ended, campaigns against abortion intensified, continuing until the turn of the century, and by 1910, almost every state had laws banning abortion.

That didn't stop women from seeking abortions, and it certainly didn't stop people from selling substances that induce abortion (also known as *abortifacients*). Advertisements for abortifacients from the late 1800s and early 1900s got around the law by using euphemisms like "relieving menstrual suppression" or "removing impurities from the system." Many women attempted to perform abortions themselves by inserting wire coat hangers or knitting needles into their vaginas, or by douching with chemicals. While some midwives advertised their services in newspaper classified pages, many people who practiced abortion were unskilled, dangerous, and coercive. Some demanded large sums of money, while others performed abortions in exchange for sex.

MRS. BIRD, Female Physician, where can be obtained Dr. Vandenburgh's Female Renovating Pills, from Germany, an effectual remedy for suppression, irregularity, and all cases where nature has stopped from any cause whatever. Sold only at Mrs. Bird's, 83 Duane st, near Broadway. n24 3m*

TO THE LADIES—Madame Costello, Female Physician, still continues to treat, with astonishing success, all diseases peculiar to females. Suppression, irregularity, obstruction, &c., by whatever cause produced, can be removed by Madame C. in a very short time. Madame C's medical establishment having undergone thorough repairs and alterations for the better accommodation of her numerous patients, she is now prepared to receive ladies on the point of confinement, or those who wish to be treated for obstruction of their monthly periods. Madame C. can be consulted at her residence, 34 Lispenard st, at all times.— All communications and letters must be post paid. 22f 1m*

HINTS TO MOTHERS for the management of their

These ads ran in the *New York Sun* in 1842. Ads like these never used the word "abortion" or "abortifacient." Instead, phrases like "suppression," "irregularity," and "obstruction of monthly periods" were used, and women were expected to read between the lines and know what they *really* meant by this. *Credit:* Library of Congress

The focus on abortion within the reproductive rights movement really didn't gain traction until the 1960s. In 1964, a woman named Gerri Santoro died while getting an illegal abortion. Although many women had suffered the same fate, her photo became the iconic symbol of the pro-choice movement. Feminists began to organize underground networks of illegal abortion providers. One group was the Jane Collective, a group of women in Chicago who were officially known as the "Abortion Counseling Service of Women's Liberation." These women created referral lists of doctors who could perform abortions, and they also taught each other how to do it themselves. A group in California called the "Army of Three" held classes on do-it-yourself abortions. Later, in 1969, an activist group called NARAL (National Abortion Rights Action League) was formed to repeal restrictive state abortion laws. Their work, along with the efforts of underground grassroots organizations, continued until the *Roe v. Wade* Supreme Court decision.

The *Roe v. Wade* decision gave women the legal right under most circumstances to make a decision about abortion, a huge victory for feminists fighting for reproductive rights. Now that abortion was legal, doctors could be trained to do it, leading to much safer outcomes. Feminists began to establish women's health clinics, which served as one-stop women's reproductive health centers providing low-cost medical services, counseling, and educational information. These health clinics maintained a political presence in the reproductive rights movement, advocating for the right to safe, accessible, low-cost abortions.

It wasn't long before "right to life" organizations began to proliferate, and efforts to restrict abortions gained momentum. These efforts involved banning Medicaid funding for abortion in most cases, passing parental notification and parental consent laws, requiring a mandatory waiting period, requiring "informed consent" (which can involve telling patients how abortion can be dangerous to one's health, as well as informing them about what's happening developmentally with their fetus), and prohibiting specific abortion techniques (such as an intact dilation and extraction abortion, otherwise known as a "partial birth abortion"). There have also been attempts to pass "personhood" laws, which would define zygotes, embryos, and fetuses as "persons" with full legal rights, and stringent regulations imposed on abortion providers, also known as TRAP regulations (Targeted Regulation of Abortion Providers). Since the *Roe v. Wade* decision, states have enacted over 1,000 restrictions on abortion—many of them passed between 2010 and 2015. And the majority of those who have been impacted by these restrictions are women of color and low-income women.

Laws haven't been the only way people have tried to ban abortions. Other tactics involve harassment, terrorism, and other forms of violence. Abortion clinics are commonly picketed and sometimes blockaded. Clinics have been bombed and set on fire. Abortion providers have been harassed, threatened, and even killed. This climate of harassment has led to a shortage of abortion clinics and well-trained abortion providers. Even though girls and women technically have the right to a safe abortion in the U.S., that right isn't easily accessible to most women.

Why do feminists fight so hard for this right? For many, it comes down to these two issues:

- Who gets to make the decision about abortion—the woman, or the government?
- Whose rights are more important—those of the fetus, or those of the woman carrying the fetus?

Not all feminists support abortion, but many feminists support the right for women to decide what's best for themselves, rather than the decision being made for them.

TRY THIS!

Have you heard of the Exquisite Uterus Project? Created by feminists and artists Helen Klebesadel and Alison Gates to raise awareness about political threats to women's reproductive rights, the Exquisite Uterus Project encourages participants to create their own expressive art piece out of an image of a uterus printed on fabric. The artwork can then be used for something functional, like a pillow or quilt. It can be something beautiful and decorative. Or it can be a direct political statement. If you visit their website at http://exquisiteuterus.com, you can see examples that others have created.

You can become an official participant of the Exquisite Uterus Project, which requires you to purchase their image printed on fabric. It's a little expensive, though, so if money is an issue, why not just create your own? I've even provided an image for you. Anyone can participate in this activity, whether or not you have a uterus.

For this activity, you'll need:

- Freezer paper
- A scanner
- A computer
- An inkjet printer
- Fabric that you can iron—strong cotton or canvas works well
- An iron and ironing board
- Scissors
- Art materials of your choice—fabric paint, fabric markers or crayons, needle and embroidery thread, cloth pieces, beads, sequins, buttons, etc.

Scan the uterus image into a computer, and save it.

Iron the piece of fabric you plan to use. Cut out an 8½″ × 11″ piece of freezer paper, place the shiny side onto the fabric, and iron it to the fabric until it sticks well. Trim the edges of the fabric so that it's exactly 8½″ × 11″. Make sure the edges of the fabric aren't frayed.

Now place the fabric in your printer tray. You want the ink to print on the fabric side, not the paper side.

Open up the uterus image on your computer, and print it. While it's printing, guide the fabric through the feeder. When it's finished, peel off your freezer paper. If you want, you can save it and reuse it, just in case you want to print another image on fabric.

If you don't have access to a computer and an inkjet printer, you can still do this activity! Take a piece of fabric and, using a pencil, copy the image of the uterus provided. Then trace over your pencil drawing with a permanent marker.

Now is the fun part! Decorate your uterus image however you like. You can color it in with fabric crayons or markers. You can paint it with fabric paint. You can create embroidery, or sew buttons, beads, or sequins onto it, or attach objects to it with fabric glue. If you want to get some ideas, visit the Exquisite Uterus Project's gallery of submissions. You'll see that there are LOTS of ways to create "uterus art"!

When you've finished, take some time to write about what the image you created means to you.

- What messages did you want to convey through your artwork?
- What feelings came up for you during this process?
- Now that you've finished your art piece, what do you want to do with it? Why?

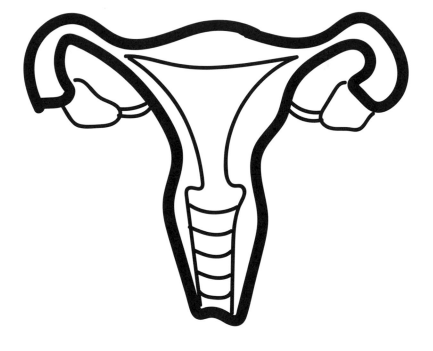

IS FOR

VIOLENCE

Emma's story:

I met Josh when I was 15. I was a sophomore, and he was a junior. He was popular, and lots of girls wanted to be his girlfriend. When he asked me out for the first time, I was on cloud nine. He made me feel pretty, and I'd never felt that way before. After school, I'd stay so I could watch his baseball practices. It was fun at first, but then my grades started slipping. But he'd get so upset if I said I wanted to go home and do my homework. Plus, I worried that if I didn't stay, he'd go find another girl. He always had tons of girls hanging around him, and that scared me.

Over time, I stopped hanging out with my friends. He made me feel guilty if I talked to anyone besides him. When baseball season was over, we'd go over to his house every day after school. I never did anything else. We'd had sex before, but a couple of times he forced me to have sex with him. He wouldn't wear a condom, even though I was terrified of getting pregnant. One time, he tried to force me to have sex, and I said no. He hit me really hard. He'd never hit me before. After that, I didn't go back to his house. But that's when it got worse.

He started texting me all day and all night. He said he was so sorry for hitting me. He sent flowers to my house. My parents thought that was so sweet, but they didn't know the whole story. He called me and left messages, and he was crying, saying that he missed me and he didn't know what he'd do without me. He also said if I didn't get back with him, he'd kill himself. That really scared me. So I did. I started going over to his house again. It was okay for a little bit, but after a while it started up all over again. He forced me to have sex with him. He wouldn't let me talk to my friends. He started hitting me more. My grades were terrible, and I got in trouble with my parents because of it. But they had no idea what was really going on.

One of my teachers asked me to stay after class to talk about my grades. I started to cry. I couldn't help it. She gave me a pamphlet about dating violence. I don't know how she knew what was going on. I finally told my parents, and they helped me get out of the situation. I changed schools and switched my cell phone number. I saw a therapist and joined a support group. I'm in college now, and I'm so grateful that I got out of that relationship.

So many girls and women have stories like this, and dating violence is increasingly common. In fact, girls and women between the ages of 16 and 24 are at the highest risk for dating violence. It can happen in both same-sex and opposite-sex relationships, and the perpetrators and victims can be any gender.

Let's look at the four major types of relationship violence: physical, verbal, psychological/emotional, and sexual.

Does your partner . . .

- Push or shove you?
- Slap or bite you?
- Kick or choke you?
- Hold you to keep you from leaving?
- Abandon you in dangerous places?
- Subject you to reckless driving?
- Threaten to hurt you with a weapon?

These are common signs of *physical abuse*. Physical abuse may not always involve being hit, kicked, or shoved. It can also involve putting your physical health and safety at risk.

Does your partner . . .

- Shout at you?
- Continually criticize you or call you names?
- Insult your family or friends?
- Ridicule or insult you because of your race, ethnicity, gender, class status, or religious beliefs?
- Humiliate you in public or private?

These are common signs of *verbal abuse*. Verbal abuse can be directed at you, or it can involve criticizing or ridiculing things that are meaningful and important to you.

Does your partner . . .

- Ignore your feelings?
- Withhold approval, appreciation, or affection as punishment?
- Control your actions, or make all your decisions for you?
- Threaten to hurt you?
- Tell you about his/her other romantic involvements?

- Act jealous?
- Manipulate you with lies and contradictions?
- Isolate you from friends and family?
- Blame you for everything?

These are common signs of *psychological* or *emotional abuse.* The goal of this form of abuse is to take away a person's sense of power and agency. It's very effective, because it causes the victim to place more trust in her partner than she does in herself.

Does your partner . . .

- Treat you as a sex object?
- Insist you dress in a more sexual way than you want to, or that you cover your body more than you want to?
- Minimize the importance of your feelings about sex?
- Criticize you sexually?
- Insist on unwanted and uncomfortable touching?
- Withhold sex and affection?
- Call you sexual names like "whore" or "frigid"?
- Force you to take off your clothes when you don't want to?
- Publicly show sexual interest in others?
- Go out with others after agreeing to a monogamous relationship?
- Force particular unwanted sex acts?

These are examples of *sexual abuse.* Again, just like with physical abuse, some forms of sexual abuse don't involve direct and unwanted sexual contact. They can, however, involve taking away a person's sexual agency, or making a person stop feeling good about sex, or using sexuality as a form of manipulation and control.

Usually dating violence doesn't start right away. In fact, many relationships start off well, and then gradually devolve into what's called the *cycle of violence.* It looks something like this:

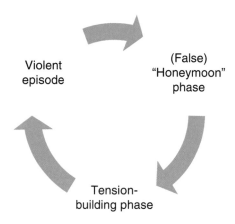

Violent episode

(False) "Honeymoon" phase

Tension-building phase

Let's use Emma's story to illustrate the three phases of the cycle of violence. When Emma first met Josh, she was happier than she'd ever been. She felt attractive and worthy, and she enjoyed spending time with Josh. That's what we call the "honeymoon" phase. But the honeymoon doesn't last, and it gradually moves into what's called the tension-building phase. Many people describe feeling like they're "walking on eggshells" when they're in this phase. They feel like if they make one false move, something bad could happen. Emma describes this early on when she wanted to go home to do her homework, rather than staying to watch Josh's baseball practices. "I worried that if I didn't stay, he'd go find another girl." That's an example of something that happens during tension-building. Eventually, the eggshells crack, and a violent episode erupts. In Emma's case, Josh forced her to have sex without a condom, and he hit her when she refused to have sex with him. When it became clear that Emma was leaving him, Josh became apologetic and begged her to come back. Now we're back to the honeymoon phase—except this time, it's a "false" honeymoon, not a real one. Because ultimately, the cycle starts all over again.

There are resources for teens to help them get out of violent relationships. Most communities have a local domestic violence agency that provides services for teens. Some schools provide education about dating violence, and some provide counseling and other services on campus. If you're unsure where to get help, a good place to start is the National Domestic Violence Hotline. You can call them at 1-800-799-7233, or you can live chat if you go to their website: http://www.thehotline.org. If you are in a violent relationship, make sure that you are in a safe place before you contact them (or any other domestic violence service), and use a computer or cell phone that your partner can't access.

Violence against girls and women is frighteningly common. But the more information you have about it, the better position you'll be in to get help if you need it.

FEMINIST HERSTORY: EVE ENSLER, THE *VAGINA MONOLOGUES*, AND ONE BILLION RISING

> *So there were vagina interviews, which became vagina monologues. Over two hundred women were interviewed. Older women, young women, married women, lesbians, single women, college professors, actors, corporate professionals, sex workers, African American women, Asian American women, Hispanic women, Native American women, Caucasian women, Jewish women. OK. At first women were reluctant to talk. They were a little shy. But once they got going, you couldn't stop them. Women secretly love to talk about their vaginas. They get very excited, mainly because no one's ever asked them before.*

That's how Eve Ensler developed *The Vagina Monologues*—through a series of conversations with women about their vaginas. Even saying the word "vagina" aloud was a groundbreaking act. And from those initial conversations, Ensler started a global movement to end violence against girls and women.

Eve Ensler was born in New York City and raised in Scarsdale, New York in a predominantly Jewish community. Throughout her childhood, Ensler was both physically and sexually abused. She didn't go public with this information until many years later. In 1994, when Ensler was 41 years old, she wrote *The Vagina Monologues*, which was originally performed as a one-woman show. Some of the monologues, such as "My Angry Vagina" and "Because He Liked to Look at It," are raucously hilarious. Others, like "The Flood," are funny, but they're also kind of depressing. There are several that are controversial, including "The Little Coochie Snorcher that Could." And a few are so painful that they're hard to listen to; "My Vagina Was My Village," for example, is based on the testimonies of women in Bosnia who were raped during the war.

The original performances of *The Vagina Monologues* generated a strong public response, which inspired Ensler to create V-Day. Every February, groups around the world are invited to perform *The Vagina Monologues* and donate the proceeds to local organizations and programs that work to end violence against women and girls. Since its inception in 1998, V-Day has raised over $100 million globally.

Since the original publication and initial performances of *The Vagina Monologues*, Ensler has added several new monologues. For example, in 2003 Ensler wrote "Under the Burqa," which addresses the plight of women in Afghanistan under the Taliban. "They Beat the Girl Out of My Boy . . . Or So They Tried," written in 2004, features a collective group of transgender women.

On February 14, 2012, Ensler launched another global movement called One Billion Rising. This call to action is based on the statistic that one in three women will be beaten or raped during her lifetime—which adds up to more than one billion women and girls worldwide. One Billion Rising events, which now take place every February, encourage survivors of sexual violence and their allies to rise up politically through art, music, marches, rallies, dancing, spoken word, and other forms of creative expression.

Some feminists and non-feminists have criticized and challenged *The Vagina Monologues*, V-Day, and One Billion Rising. Colleges and universities with religious affiliations, such as Gonzaga University in Spokane, Washington, refused to perform *The Vagina Monologues*. (Gonzaga eventually lifted the ban, and its first performance was in 2011.) In other cases, groups have challenged *The Vagina Monologues* for not being trans-inclusive enough. In 2015, Mount Holyoke College, an all-women's college in Massachusetts, cancelled its performance of *The Vagina Monologues* for that reason. A student representative who fought to ban *The Vagina Monologues* said this:

> *At its core, the show offers an extremely narrow perspective on what it means to be a woman. Gender is a wide and varied experience, one that cannot simply be reduced to biological or anatomical distinctions, and many of us who have participated in the show have grown increasingly uncomfortable presenting material that is inherently reductionist and exclusive.*

Eve Ensler made a rebuttal statement in *Time* magazine several days after the decision was made at Mount Holyoke:

> The Vagina Monologues *never intended to be a play about what it means to be a woman. It is and always has been a play about what it means to have a vagina. In the play, I never defined a woman as a person with a vagina.*

The Vagina Monologues still sparks tension and debate within the transgender community and among feminists of all gender identities. And yet, that's a sign that Ensler's activism has created a cultural conversation and call to action. What does it mean to be a woman? What does it mean to have (or not to have) a vagina? Why are so many women—and vaginas—around the world so horrifically mistreated and oppressed? Those are important conversations, and they all demand action.

TRY THIS!

This exercise is best done in a group. You could do this activity in an afterschool club, with your friends, or with teens in a community group. You could also share this activity with a teacher whom you think might be open to it.

For this exercise, you'll need:

- A stack of 8½ × 11 inch paper, with each sheet cut in half
- Pens
- A trash can

Before we start, let's talk about three types of losses that people can experience:

- *Predictable losses*, which are losses that you choose or expect;
- *Random losses*, which are losses that you might not want, but happen because of your choices or circumstances; and
- *Random and unpredictable losses*, which are losses that someone else chooses for you.

Violence causes injury, and those injuries can be physical, psychological, material, or relational. In each of those cases, injuries caused by violence result in losses—an inevitable result of oppression. So let's talk about losses, and how oppression can lead to all three types discussed above.

Give everyone sixteen sheets of paper, and ask each person to divide them into sets of four. Everyone should do the following:

- On the first four sheets, write down the names of four **people** that you love.
- On the second four sheets, write down four **things** that are important to you.
- On the third four sheets, write down four **ideas** that you value.
- On the fourth four sheets, write down four **places** you've been that you never want to forget.

When everyone is finished, ask each person to choose one item from each category (people, things, ideas, places), crumple the papers into a ball, and throw them away. These represent predictable losses.

Now, ask everyone to turn the papers in each category face down, so no one can see what's written on them. Ask each person, without looking, to choose one item from each category (people, things, ideas, places), crumple the papers into a ball, and throw them away. These represent random losses.

Ask everyone to keep their papers face down so that they can't see what is written on them. At this point, you (or whoever the facilitator is) should go to each participant, choose one item from each category (people, things, ideas, places), crumple the papers into a ball, and throw them away. These represent random and unpredictable losses.

Ask each person to turn the remaining four sheets back over. What's left? Have a conversation about how each person feels about what is left, and what was taken away.

When a person is a victim of violence and oppression, losses are inevitable. Some of those losses might be predictable. The vast majority, however, tend to be random and unpredictable. Have a discussion with the group about the losses that occur as a result of sexism, racism, class oppression, LGBT oppression, and, of course, violence.

W IS FOR

WOMAN TROUBLE

Take out a piece of paper. Write down as many phrases that you can think of that describe "being on your period," without using the words "period" or "menstruation." Go!

I bet that wasn't hard.

I've got the curse.
I'm on the rag.
I got a visit from Aunt Flo.
I'm surfing the Crimson Tide.
I've got the Red Dot special.
It's Shark Week.

It's amazing, really, how many ways we can talk about menstruation without saying "menstruation." It's almost like the word is poisonous. It's certainly taboo to talk about anything menstruation-related in an obvious way. Rarely do we see menstruation portrayed on television or in the movies, and when we do, it's often framed as a humiliating experience. Stephen King's *Carrie* is a perfect example, and one of the few cinematic portrayals of menstruation. When Carrie gets her period for the first time in the locker room shower, the other girls throw tampons and sanitary pads at her. Later, at prom, one of the girls dumps a bucket of pig's blood on her. No wonder girls and women go to such great lengths to hide the fact that they're on their period.

Where do these menstrual taboos come from? In many religious traditions, menstrual blood is viewed as "ritually unclean." As a result, girls and women have been quarantined in menstrual huts during their periods. They've been prohibited from entering sanctuary spaces. Some religions say that sexual activity during a woman's period is forbidden. Even sharing food with a menstruating female, or allowing her to prepare food, has been seen as unsanitary. Most people don't engage in these practices anymore, but a few religious traditions continue to treat menstruation as a pollutant.

Often, stereotypical beliefs emerge out of fear and ignorance, and menstrual taboos are a perfect example of this. In ancient times, and throughout many mythological traditions, moon goddesses were worshipped and revered, for they had the power to create and nurture life. But people also believed that moon goddesses possessed a feminine power that, if unchecked, could spiral out of control. At that time, people didn't really understand the biological basis of menstruation—how could a woman bleed so heavily, once a month, and not be injured or dying? People came to fear menstrual blood, and menstruating women in general, which boiled down to two major reactions:

1. People leaned on superstitions to explain what they didn't understand. In this case, people started associating the menstrual cycle with the lunar cycle. If women menstruated every 28 days, and the lunar cycle occurred over 28 days, they must be related, right? (Note: just because two things happen at the same time doesn't mean that one caused the other.)

2. People attempted to contain the cause of their fears. They did this in lots of ways. One way was to label menstruating women as "crazy." The word "lunatic," interestingly, has its roots in menstrual fears (luna = moon). If a menstruating woman is considered to be a lunatic, then something needs to be done about her, right? Usually, she was contained and separated from the general population. That's where menstrual tents/huts and prohibitions against entering certain spaces originated.

Essentially, people feared menstruation because they thought it was all-powerful. Isn't that fascinating? And now, many thousands of years later, we still fear menstruation. We don't want to talk about it, and we certainly don't want to see it. And yet, the ability to generate and nurture life is probably the most powerful human feat in the universe, and it takes a uterus to be able to do that. A woman's most powerful biological process is the thing we most want to suppress.

These menstrual taboos exist everywhere. Among some tribes in India and in parts of sub-Saharan Africa, girls who start their period might have to give up going to school. This is partly because of menstrual fears. As mentioned, in some parts of the world women are kept isolated while on their period, and forced to live in a hut or a shed. But much of this is because of lack of access to good feminine hygiene supplies and practices. Girls and women who don't have access to sanitary pads and tampons, clean running water, or clean and safe bathroom facilities are more likely to experience health problems and are more likely to stop their education. In fact, studies have shown a significant link between access to good menstrual hygiene and access to education.

The United States isn't immune to these issues. The number one item homeless and unhoused women request is feminine hygiene products. They may not be able to afford them, or they might not purchase a pack of sanitary pads because they're too bulky to carry around. Homeless shelters may not have feminine hygiene products on hand, because people don't often donate them. For that matter, finding a clean bathroom and shower facility can be a challenge. All of this can lead to infections and other health issues.

Recently, feminists have been bringing menstruation out in the open. Some have started social media campaigns like #TheHomeless Period, which educates people about menstrual issues among homeless women, and #FreeTheTampons, which is an advocacy effort to get free tampons and sanitary pads in public restrooms. Others lobbied for an end to the "tampon tax," an effort spearheaded by a bill introduced to the California legislature in early 2016. Cristina Garcia, co-author of the bill, said this in a press release:

> *Fundamentally this is about gender equity and leveling the field. Every month, for 40 years of our lives, we are taxed for being born women. Every month of our adult life we are taxed for our biology. Every month we are told our periods are a luxury, while also being told they are something to be ashamed of and we must hide. Let me be clear, on biology, periods are not luxuries and they are definitely not something women should be ashamed of, period!*

The governor of California vetoed the bill. However, there's a silver lining: because of that bill, other states have jumped on the bandwagon to eliminate the "tampon tax." The governor of New York, for example, recently signed legislation that abolishes taxes on feminine hygiene products. A woman in Tampa, Florida filed a class-action lawsuit designed to repeal the "tampon tax" and offer tax refunds to customers. And ten other states don't have a tampon tax at all (including those states that don't have sales tax).

Girls and women are talking openly and unapologetically about menstruation, that's for sure. And that's a good thing.

FEMINIST HERSTORY: GLORIA STEINEM AND *MS.* MAGAZINE

What if men could menstruate? Would that change how people react to it? Would they be more accepting of, even embracing and celebrating, this natural bodily process? Gloria Steinem, in 1978, asked herself that very question—and here's how she answered it:

> *So what would happen if suddenly, magically, men could menstruate and women could not?*
>
> *Clearly, menstruation would become an enviable, worthy, masculine event:*
>
> *Men would brag about how long and how much.*
>
> *Young boys would talk about it as the envied beginning of manhood. Gifts, religious ceremonies, family dinners, and stag parties would mark the day.*
>
> . . .
>
> *Sanitary supplies would be federally funded and free. Of course, some men would still pay for the prestige of such commercial brands as Paul Newman Tampons, Muhammad Ali's Rope-a-Dope Pads, John Wayne Maxi Pads, and Joe Namath Jock Shields—"For Those Light Bachelor Days."*
>
> *Statistical surveys would show that men did better in sports and won more Olympic medals during their periods.*
>
> . . .
>
> *Street guys would invent slang ("He's a three-pad man") and "give fives" on the corner with some exchange like, "Man you lookin' good!"*
>
> *"Yeah, man, I'm on the rag!"*

Hilarious, right? And yet, the fact that this satirical piece still resonates today is sobering. Let's learn more about the woman who wrote this groundbreaking piece.

Steinem was born on March 25, 1934 in Toledo, Ohio. Her paternal grandmother, Pauline Perlmutter Steinem, had immigrated to the United States after rescuing many of her family members during the Holocaust. After arriving in the U.S., Pauline became involved in women's rights and the suffrage movement; she was chairwoman of the education committee of the National Woman Suffrage Association, and a delegate to the 1908 International Council of Women. Steinem's parents divorced when she was ten, and afterwards she had to take care of her mother, who suffered from delusions and violent outbursts, and who was frequently in and out of mental hospitals. Seeing how her mother was treated within the mental health system woke Steinem up to the realities of sexism and misogyny, and set the foundation for her feminist consciousness.

After graduating high school, Steinem studied government at Smith College, graduating magna cum laude. Afterwards, she traveled to India on a research fellowship, where she learned the basics of grassroots activism. Later, she moved to New York and began her career as a freelance journalist. Her first "big story" was an exposé of the Playboy Club, where she went undercover and posed as a Playboy Bunny. Being a Playboy Bunny, according to her research, was anything but glamorous and cushy; in contrast, Steinem's report revealed a number of exploitative practices in the workplace. Despite the fact that this article generated national attention, Steinem had difficulty finding journalism assignments—partly because she was a woman, and partly because she reported on the "fluffy" and "sensationalistic" topic of Playboy Bunnies. Finally, in 1968, she became a founding editor at *New York* magazine, where she reported on a wide range of social and political issues.

One of her first assignments at *New York* magazine involved attending an abortion speak-out, and something clicked for Steinem that day. Three years earlier, when Steinem was 22 years old, she herself had had an abortion, and she heard things at this speak-out that radicalized her and spurred her to action. Years later, Steinem had this to say about her epiphany:

> *It [abortion] is supposed to make us a bad person. But I must say, I never felt that. I used to sit and try and figure out how old the child would be, trying to make myself feel guilty. But I never could! I think the person who said: 'Honey, if men could get pregnant, abortion would be a sacrament' was right. Speaking for myself, I knew it was the first time I had taken responsibility for my own life. I wasn't going to let things happen to me. I was going to direct my life, and therefore it felt positive. But still, I didn't tell anyone. Because I knew that out there it wasn't [positive].*

Shortly afterwards, Steinem began participating in feminist rallies, sit-ins, protests, and other forms of activism. In 1971, Steinem and her colleague Dorothy Pitman Hughes co-founded *Ms.* magazine, which started as an insert in *New York*. It sold out within days, and in 1972, it became an independent magazine. The same year *Ms.* was founded, she and a group of feminists, including Bella Abzug, Shirley Chisholm, and Betty Friedan, formed the National Women's Political Caucus to increase the number of women involved in the political system. At that founding meeting, Steinem delivered her "Address to the Women of America," which is now considered one of the greatest speeches of the 20th century.

Today, Steinem continues to advocate for women's rights. And *Ms.* magazine is still in publication.

TRY THIS!

Periods are largely invisible in our culture. So few cultural references to menstruation exist, and the ones that do aren't very positive or empowering. But in the music world, especially in the punk/alternative rock scenes, periods are out, loud, and proud. In this activity, you're going to delve into this world of period empowerment—by creating a period playlist! (And yours will be better than the one Ashton Kutcher's character created in *No Strings Attached*.)

For this activity, you'll need:

- A computer or smartphone
- Access to a music service, like Spotify or iTunes

Below are some songs that are about periods. (Really! They do exist.) Search for each of these songs on your music service, and spend some time listening to them.

Songs About Periods (or Blood!)
- "Bachelorette" by Björk
- "PMS" by Mary J. Blige
- "Trying" by Bully
- "Blood Red Summer" by Coheed and Cambria
- "Period Piece" by Lena D
- "Blood in the Boardroom" by Ani DiFranco
- "My Red Self" by Heavens to Betsy
- "Feedback" by Janet Jackson
- "PMS Blues" by Dolly Parton
- "Ophelia" by Kinnie Starr
- "Crimson Wave" by Tacocat

Now, here's another list of songs that aren't necessarily about periods, but are generally feminist and empowering. Some girls and women don't feel so great about themselves while they're menstruating (or right before their period starts). These songs might offer a good pick-me-up during those times, reminding you of the power you carry within yourself.

Songs that are Awesome and Empowering
- "Beautiful" by Christina Aguilera
- "Can't Hold Us Down" by Christina Aguilera
- "Run the World (Girls)" by Beyoncé
- "Rebel Girl" by Bikini Kill
- "Try" by Colbie Caillat
- "Independent Women Part 1" by Destiny's Child
- "Bad Reputation" by Joan Jett and the Blackhearts
- "Girl on Fire" by Alicia Keys
- "Hot Topic" by Le Tigre
- "Just a Girl" by No Doubt
- "Roar" by Katy Perry
- "Perfect" by Pink
- "U.N.I.T.Y." by Queen Latifah
- "Expression" by Salt 'N Pepa
- "When I Was a Boy" by Dar Williams

Note the songs you like. Why do they appeal to you? What messages do you get from listening to these songs? How do they make you feel?

Feel free to add any songs you want! These are just some suggestions, many of which live outside the mainstream playlists. Add any songs that help you tap into your inner strength and power.

IS FOR

XL

"I'm sorry. We don't carry that in your size."

That's the last thing girls and women want to hear when they go shopping. Unfortunately, far too many of us hear exactly that. Many girls and women in the U.S. hate their bodies. They go to great lengths to try to lose weight and look a certain way. According to one study, more than half of girls between age 6 and 8 think their ideal weight is thinner than their current size. By age 7, 1 in 4 children has engaged in dieting behavior.

These statistics are alarming, but not all that surprising. The reality is that we live in an incredibly fat-phobic and fat-hating culture. Girls and women are bombarded with the message that thin is beautiful, and fat is ugly and shameful. These messages are reinforced by things like "thinspiration" and "pro-ana" anorexia blogs—sites that provide "support" for girls who want to get thin and stay thin. In the movies, we repeatedly see thin characters that are good and smart, and fat characters that are evil (like Ursula in *The Little Mermaid*), silly and unintelligent (like Pumbaa in *The Lion King*), or the butt of other people's jokes (think Fat Amy in *Pitch Perfect*).

But anti-fat attitudes go far beyond the media. Girls and women who are plus-size are more likely than their thin counterparts to experience prejudice and discrimination. Despite the fact that the average women's clothing size in the U.S. is 14 (which is plus-size in most stores), the average women's clothing store—including Anthropologie, Express, American Apparel, Urban Outfitters, and Abercrombie & Fitch—doesn't carry that size in their stores. In fact, in the modeling world, size 6 is considered to be "plus-size." Girls who are overweight are more likely to be bullied in school. Women who are plus-size are more likely to experience housing, job, and health care discrimination, and are more prone to health problems because of the stress of dealing with anti-fat stigma.

How do you live in a culture like this and not internalize body hatred? It's hard. Think of all the derogatory words that exist to describe female body fat: *Muffin top. Poochy tummy. Bra bulge. Cankles. Back fat.* Instead, what do girls want? A thigh gap. No wonder over half of teenage girls try to lose weight by skipping meals, fasting, smoking cigarettes, vomiting, and taking laxatives—all of which are unhealthy, and many of which may be signs of an eating disorder.

Because of these dangerous weight and body image ideals, many feminists have become involved in efforts to end body shame. One of the approaches feminists have embraced is called Health at Every Size (HAES). Instead of pressuring girls and women to lose weight and achieve an unrealistic body ideal, the HAES approach helps girls accept their bodies, and helps them find ways of taking care of themselves. HAES includes the following components:

- **Respect.** This includes respect for your own body, as well as respect for body diversity.
- **Compassionate self-care.** This involves learning to eat in a way that's healthy and enjoyable, as well as finding joy in being physically active in whatever way feels good.

- **Critical awareness.** This component teaches girls and women to challenge assumptions about body image and health (such as the idea that "thinness = perfect health"). It also teaches us to be aware of our bodies, and to trust what our bodies are telling us.

FEMINIST HERSTORY: THE FAT ACCEPTANCE MOVEMENT AND FEMINISM

Size discrimination is real. According to one study, compared to thin women, fat women are more likely to be perceived as lazy, slow, undisciplined, and sloppy. And size discrimination has tangible effects. Fat people often face barriers to receiving medical care. They experience job discrimination, earning less than their thin counterparts. They frequently have a history of being bullied in childhood, which affects their self-esteem. And, in most places in the U.S., they don't have any legal protections. It's perfectly legal to fire (or not hire) someone because of their weight.

Sound familiar? Many of these issues overlap with feminist concerns. In the 1970s, at the height of the second wave of feminism, a group of women in Los Angeles saw those parallels and began to take action.

Sara Fishman was one of those women. One day, when she was at the Hollywood Public Library, she picked up a book written by Llewellyn Louderback called *Fat Power*. Even though it sat alongside a wide range of diet books, this book was clearly different, and Fishman was intrigued. The book's argument rested on three different concepts:

- On average, fat people don't eat more than thin people.
- Diets don't work.
- Fat people who are free from discrimination are at a lower risk for heart disease, hypertension, and other health issues commonly associated with being fat.

Doing further research into these claims galvanized Fishman into action. She and a group of women started the Fat Underground, a feminist political action group committed to educating people about fat oppression and ending discrimination against fat people. In 1973, Fishman and Judy Freespirit published the Fat Liberation Manifesto, which outlined the Fat Underground's mission and made a clear declaration of activism. In 1981, psychoanalyst Susie Orbach published her now-classic book *Fat Is a Feminist Issue*, and in 1983, members of the Fat Underground published *Shadow on a Tightrope: Writings by Women on Fat Oppression*. In 1984, *Radiance* magazine was launched, which was the first women's magazine to feature fat women in a positive, empowering way. The feminist fat acceptance movement had begun.

Fat activism continued into the 1990s and dovetailed with the third wave of feminism. The first International No Diet Day was held

This is the first issue of the 'zine *Fat!So?* The image on the cover is of "healthy, normal, human fat cells." 'Zines from the 1990s often had a DIY aesthetic to them. They were often illustrated by hand and bound with staples. *Credit: Fat!So?* 'zine cover (1994), cover photo by Donald W. Fawcett, MD in 1992, and it continues to be observed every May. The National Organization for Women made an official statement against size discrimination, and initiated a body image task force. Feminists began publishing fat feminist zines, the most popular of which was Marilyn Wann's *Fat!So?: for people who don't apologize for their size*. In 1998, Wann expanded her zine into a book, titled *Fat!So? Because You Don't Have to Apologize for Your Size*. This became the go-to book in the third-wave feminist fat acceptance movement.

Some people, particularly medical researchers and practitioners, criticize the fat acceptance movement for ignoring research linking obesity to a range of health issues. And yet, fat acceptance is still a prominent voice in the cultural conversation about obesity. Several cities, including Washington, DC; San Francisco and Santa Cruz, CA; Madison, WI; and Binghamton, NY, have passed laws prohibiting discrimination based on a person's weight. As of this writing, only Michigan has passed similar legislation statewide. Medical practitioners are becoming more aware of the dangers of yo-yo dieting and extreme weight loss and courses in Fat Studies, analogous to Women and Gender Studies, Queer Studies, and Ethnic Studies, are being offered at a number of colleges and universities.

Fat Liberation Manifesto
by Sara Fishman and Judy Freespirit

1. WE *believe that fat people are fully entitled to human respect and recognition.*
2. WE *are angry at mistreatment by commercial and sexist interests. These have exploited our bodies as objects of ridicule, thereby creating an immensely profitable market selling the false promise of avoidance of, or relief from, that ridicule.*
3. WE *see our struggle as allied with the struggles of other oppressed groups against classism, racism, sexism, ageism, financial exploitation, imperialism and the like.*

4. WE demand equal rights for fat people in all aspects of life, as promised in the Constitution of the United States. We demand equal access to goods and services in the public domain, and an end to discrimination against us in the areas of employment, education, public facilities and health services.

5. WE single out as our special enemies the so-called "reducing" industries. These include diet clubs, reducing salons, fat farms, diet doctors, diet books, diet foods and food supplements, surgical procedures, appetite suppressants, drugs and gadgetry such as wraps and "reducing machines".

WE demand that they take responsibility for their false claims, acknowledge that their products are harmful to the public health, and publish long-term studies proving any statistical efficacy of their products. We make this demand knowing that over 99% of all weight loss programs, when evaluated over a five-year period, fail utterly, and also knowing the extreme proven harmfulness of frequent large changes in weight.

6. WE repudiate the mystified "science" which falsely claims that we are unfit. It has both caused and upheld discrimination against us, in collusion with the financial interests of insurance companies, the fashion and garment industries, reducing industries, the food and drug industries, and the medical and psychiatric establishment.

7. WE refuse to be subjugated to the interests of our enemies. We fully intend to reclaim power over our bodies and our lives. We commit ourselves to pursue these goals together.

TRY THIS!

So many girls and women have a negative body image. This activity is designed to help you focus on the positive. For this activity, you'll need these materials:

- A roll of butcher paper
- Tape

- A pencil
- A stack of magazines
- Scissors
- Glue sticks
- Other art supplies (crayons, colored pencils, markers, paint— you choose!)
- A friend you trust

Get a large piece of butcher paper, and tape it down to the floor. Lie down on your back, on top of the butcher paper, and ask your friend to trace your body. Now, do the same for your friend.

Now, you're going to create art within the outline of your body. You can use any art materials you want. Draw or collage images that show what you like about your body. Add descriptive words like *strong, flexible, soft,* or *powerful*: words that reflect positive qualities about your body and the wonderful things your body can do. Don't include judgments or criticism—we're focusing on what's good and valuable about your body. By the end of this exercise, the entire area within the outline of your body should be covered with words, images, and artwork.

Did you struggle with any parts of your body? If so, what positive attributes were you able to come up with? How did it feel to focus only on the positive? If you feel comfortable, share your responses with your friend, and ask your friend to share responses with you. If this feels too vulnerable, take some time to journal about the experience.

IS FOR

YIN-YANG

Have you ever seen this symbol before?

I bet you have. Do you know what it means?

Although it's become quite trendy and fashionable, the yin-yang symbol is a fundamental component of Chinese philosophy. The black and white intertwining curves symbolize complementary opposites, such as cold/hot, dark/light, moon/sun—and feminine/masculine.

To be a bit more specific, the black area, which is Yin, represents:

- darkness,
- passivity,

- intuition,
- cold,
- softness,
- stillness,
- weakness, and
- submission.

The white area, which is Yang, symbolizes:

- light,
- activity,
- logic,
- heat,
- firmness,
- movement,
- strength, and
- dominance.

Black and white. Cold and hot. Weakness and strength. Pure opposites. Which is exactly how we perceive males and females in our culture—as polar opposites. What's interesting is that, despite these cultural perceptions, the reality is quite different. Boys and girls are actually more similar than different.

You're probably thinking, *Whaaaat????* But hear me out.

Some gender differences definitely exist. The biggest one is that males tend to have more physical strength and athletic ability than females. (Although now that girls and women have more opportunities to participate in athletics, they've been catching up.) But other than that, differences between boys and girls are actually quite small, or non-existent. Boys and girls don't differ much in overall math and verbal ability. They also aren't very different when it comes to assertiveness and self-esteem. Even height differences, when you compare averages, aren't significant. These findings aren't new—in fact, they're well-documented by social science researchers.

So why do people believe that boys and girls are so different, even though the evidence tells us something else? The idea of gender differences may appeal to our gut, instinctual sense; it just *feels* right that boys and girls are different, right? It's also way more exciting to think about differences than it is to acknowledge similarities. "Study Shows No Difference between Boys' and Girls' School Performance" isn't a headline that will sell magazines and newspapers. But "Study Shows Girls Excel in School, While Boys Lag" grabs your attention, doesn't it?

Believing in gender differences just because you feel it in your heart is dangerous. These beliefs can result in several outcomes:

- **They contribute to the *confirmation bias*.** If you believe something is true, you're more likely to notice things that confirm your belief, and less likely to notice (or give credit to) things that contradict it. That's called the confirmation bias. People believe in gender differences, and then they see them everywhere.
- **They create a self-fulfilling prophecy.** If you're a girl, and you think that girls aren't confident leaders, that belief can actually undermine your confidence and leadership skills. That phenomenon is called *stereotype threat*.
- **They create an "other-fulfilling" prophecy.** Studies have shown that, to some extent, people tend to become what others think of them. One of my students, Priscilla, had a math teacher who told her she didn't have a "math personality" (whatever that means). Not surprisingly, she did poorly in that class and had to re-take it. The next time, she had a different teacher, who was much more supportive and encouraging—and that time, Priscilla earned a B in the class.

- **They contribute to non-intersectional thinking.** When we focus on differences between "girls" and "boys," or "women" and "men," it's easy to assume that we're talking about "all girls" and "all boys," or "all women" and "all men." In reality, there tend to be more differences *among* girls and *among* boys than between girls and boys. Let's look at an example:

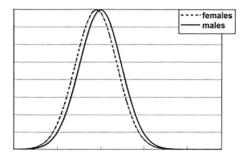

Published in the *American Psychologist* in September 2005, this graph was created by a psychologist named Janet Shibley Hyde, who developed the "gender similarities hypothesis." The X axis represents self-esteem scores, and the Y axis represents the number of participants. Most participants score at the midpoint of self-esteem scores, while fewer participants score at the extremes, regardless of gender.

This graph represents differences in self-esteem scores between females and males. If you're looking strictly at differences, on average, males tend to have higher self-esteem scores than females. But you can see from this graph that there is an enormous amount of overlap between the two groups. Essentially, males and females are more similar than different, and there are more differences within each group than between the two groups.

- **They contribute to binary thinking.** Our culture loves boxes and categories, especially when there are only two of them. Male or female. Black or white. Rich or poor. But gender isn't really a binary system: it's more like a continuum. There are certainly a lot of people who identify as male or female, but we also know that some people identify as intersex, transgender, genderqueer, gender-fluid, and a whole host of other identities that lie between "male" and "female."

Here's a healthier (and more culturally accurate) way of thinking about the yin-yang symbol: That image is meant to represent balance, harmony, and wholeness. It embodies the idea that we can't be healthy and complete if the scales are tipped strongly in one direction or another. Girls and boys who strike a balance between strength and weakness, logical thinking and intuition, stillness and activity, and, yes, masculinity and femininity, tend to be well-adjusted and confident—more so than their peers who are strongly gender-typed.

FEMINIST HERSTORY: A HISTORY OF SEX DIFFERENCE RESEARCH

Imagine that you're conducting a psychological study for a science fair, and all the students in your class have agreed to participate. You ask the boys to form one line, and the girls to form another. Then you take out a tape measure, and, starting with the boys, you measure each participant's head circumference. You calculate the average circumference among the boys, compare that number to the average circumference among the girls, and discover that the boys have bigger heads than the girls. In your science fair report, you conclude that because boys have bigger heads than girls, they must have bigger brains, and therefore the boys must be smarter than the girls. Do you think you'd win a science fair award for this study?

Of course, this is a ridiculous study. And I wish I could say that I came up with the idea of this fictional study on my own, but I didn't. In fact, this was an actual study conducted in 1887 by a scientist named George Romanes. Back then, it was generally accepted without question that men were more intelligent than women. As a result, it was easy for Romanes to investigate a research question based on assumptions that he *thought* were true, but never really questioned. Here's what's really scary: it wasn't until 1979 that studies were published demonstrating that human brain size (or human head size, for that matter) had nothing to do with intelligence.

Most people have never heard of George Romanes, but I bet you've heard of Charles Darwin, especially if you've studied the principles of evolution and natural selection. In 1871, Darwin wrote a book titled *The Descent of Man, and Selection in Relation to Sex*, which outlined how psychological traits evolve through the process of sexual selection. This theory has been used to explain why men use one set of strategies to attract women, and women used a completely different set of strategies to attract men. (This, of course, assumes that men aren't attracted to men and women aren't attracted to women.) Here's how the theory goes.

First, according to Darwin, there's a basic biological difference between males and females: Males produce sperm, and females produce eggs. Sperm is essentially unlimited—males have the capacity to produce sperm from puberty until the day they die. They can also ejaculate and release sperm whenever they want to. But eggs, in contrast, eventually run out—females start ovulating during adolescence, and they stop when they hit menopause. And they can't release eggs on demand—there's a short window of opportunity (just a couple of days per month) for an egg to be fertilized by a sperm. That basic biological difference, according to Darwin, gives rise to sex differences in courtship and sexual behaviors.

How does that work? Let's start with males. If the goal of the human species is to reproduce, and if males can produce unlimited amounts of sperm, then it might be in his best interest to try to impregnate as many females as possible. Because of that, according to Darwin, males probably won't just stick with one female. Instead, they'll try to "spread their seed" as much as possible, and the best way to do that is to be non-monogamous. If multiple males are competing for the same female, those males are likely to be aggressive towards each other. Since only one male can impregnate a female at a time, each male wants to be "the one," and usually it'll be the strongest and most aggressive one (the one who wins the fight). Males might, on occasion, become aggressive towards females. If she doesn't want to have sex with him, he might force her to—because if the goal of the human species is reproduction, what the female wants doesn't really matter.

Okay. Breathe. We'll unpack this in a few minutes. But first, let's talk about what Darwin had to say about females and sexual behaviors.

Remember that, compared to males, females have a limited set of eggs, and those eggs aren't available 24/7. Because of that, according to Darwin, females can't afford to waste their eggs on just any old guy. She won't go on the hunt for a mate—instead, she'll wait for a suitable mate to come to her. She'll probably be finicky about her choice of mate, because if she wants to ensure that her offspring will survive, she'll want to choose the best available mate so her offspring will get the best genes possible. Once she finds a suitable mate, she'll "stand by her man" and stick with him through thick and thin. She knows, of course, that a good man is hard to find, and once she finds one, she's going to hang onto him for as long as possible.

Does this sound sexist to you at all? It should, because it is. Darwin's theory reinforces simplistic gender stereotypes (males are aggressive and competitive, females are passive and loyal). It also comes dangerously close to justifying rape and sexual assault—after all, males are wired to behave like this, right? Most importantly, the biggest challenge to this theory is that there's little evidence to support it. Humans, both male and female, engage in a range of sexual behaviors for a wide variety of reasons, and reproduction is only one of those reasons—and so do animals for that matter. There's no one prototypical sexual strategy that occurs consistently across all animal species. Yet, because Darwin's theory reflects common beliefs about gender and sexuality, people tend to accept it because it "feels right."

But in the world of science "feeling right" doesn't cut it as evidence. In 1875, shortly after Darwin wrote *The Descent of Man, and Selection in Relation to Sex*, an abolitionist and suffragette named Antoinette Brown Blackwell published a scathing critique of Darwin's sex difference theories. Her book, titled *The Sexes Throughout Nature*, argued that equality between men and women was an evolutionary necessity, and that survival of the species depended on it. Unfortunately, her work was completely dismissed by the scientific community, and it took more than a century for evolutionary theorists to revisit the idea of sex differences due to evolution. Even so, many scholars in the field of evolution still accept these theories.

One notable exception is Sarah Blaffer Hrdy, an anthropologist and primatologist at the University of California at Davis. She is one of the leading scientists to provide a feminist reinterpretation of evolutionary theory. In 1999 she wrote a book titled *Mother Nature: Maternal Instincts and How They Shape the Human Species*, in which she challenges several of Darwin's beliefs about sex differences. She debunks the idea of the "maternal instinct," arguing that responsiveness to one's young depends on a variety of factors. She also presents the concept of cooperative breeding and "alloparenting," which essentially reflects the idea that, instead of one primary caregiver, "it takes a village to raise a child." In many ways, her contributions to the field of evolutionary psychology have challenged people's assumptions about innate sex differences.

TRY THIS!

This activity is very powerful if you can do it with a group, although you can do it by yourself as well. Either way, each participant will need the following materials:

- A pen or pencil
- A notebook
- A printed copy of the yin-yang symbol
- A black colored pencil and a white colored pencil
- Masking tape (if doing with a group)

For each participant:

Make a list of adjectives that define your personality. Are you quiet, bold, introspective, bookish, impulsive, creative, daring, shy, animated, humble? Write all of them down.

Now, identify which adjectives feel more "yin," and which feel more "yang." Using the white colored pencil, write the "yin" adjectives within the dark part of the symbol. Then, using the black colored pencil, write the "yang" adjectives within the light part of the symbol. Don't write your name on the paper with the yin-yang symbol—only write the adjectives.

Ask each person to reflect on these questions:

- How balanced is your personality between yin and yang?
- Do you have an equal number of adjectives on each side, or is one side more heavily weighted than the other?

If you're doing this activity in a larger group, tape each participant's yin-yang symbol to the wall, and invite participants to come look at them. Is it easy to tell which symbols were created by a girl, and which ones were created by a boy? Do you see sharp differences between girls and boys, or is there diversity within each group? Use these questions to facilitate a group discussion about similarities and differences.

ZERO

"When a girl wants to diet herself into a size zero, she is aspiring to become nothing."
—Jean Kilbourne

"Just as she is entering womanhood, eager to spread her wings, to become truly sexually active, empowered, independent—the culture moves in to cut her down to size."
—Jean Kilbourne

Both of these quotes have stuck with me for a long time. They remind me of various girls I've known when we were eight, nine, ten years old, feisty and adventurous girls who felt like they could take on the world and do anything they set their mind to. And then

I thought about what happens for so many girls during adolescence. They start to doubt themselves. They become self-conscious. They scrutinize their bodies and their appearance. They dial back their voices, or stop speaking up altogether.

Then I thought about all of the problems that adolescent girls in America risk facing. Low self-esteem. Changes in academic performance, particularly in math. Date rape and dating violence. Body image concerns. Eating disorders. Drug and alcohol use. Cigarette smoking. Teen pregnancy. Sexually transmitted infections and diseases. Cutting and other forms of self-harm. When the example of cutting came to mind, I recall closing my eyes and imagining a bird getting ready to take flight—and a big, amorphous mass swooping in and clipping her wings.

That image has stuck with me ever since, and it's why I wanted to write this book. Girls and women have so much power, and our culture continues to take that power away from us. But feminism gives us a mighty and formidable set of tools to help us reclaim our power, to help us unclip our wings and allow us to spread them as far as we possibly can.

All of this got me thinking . . .

How much energy do girls and women use up by:

- Trying to lose weight and achieve an unrealistically thin body ideal?
- Suppressing and silencing their voices?
- Engaging in self-destructive behaviors?
- Trying to become nothing?

What if girls and women used that energy to create equity and justice for all?

What if girls and women were to "take back the Zero"? What goals would we set for ourselves?

Imagine the possibilities.

Zero gender stereotypes.
Zero body shame.
Zero eating disorders.
Zero feminine-bashing.
Zero sex-negativity.
Zero boundary violations.
Zero gender violence.
Zero sexualization of girls.
Zero bullying.
Zero racism.
Zero homophobia.
Zero transphobia.
Zero educational limits.
Zero career limits.
Zero gender achievement gaps.
Zero wage gaps.
Zero self-esteem issues.
Zero self-hatred.

Imagine if all that energy were to be used to create a new reality. Imagine if the possibilities were infinite.

FEMINIST HERSTORY: CORAZON AQUINO AND THE 1986 PEOPLE POWER REVOLUTION

On October 19, 2016, millions of people tuned in to watch the final presidential debate between Democratic nominee Hillary Clinton and Republican nominee Donald Trump. The 2016 presidential campaign had been one of the most divisive and contested in history. Prior to the debate, recordings from the tabloid show *Access*

Hollywood of Donald Trump making vulgar comments about women had been publicly released. That, combined with the image of Donald Trump looming menacingly behind Hillary Clinton during the second presidential debate, was fresh in viewers' minds as they watched this final contest.

Towards the end of the debate, moderator Chris Wallace directed a question about Social Security to Hillary Clinton. This was her response:

> *Well, Chris, I am on record as saying that we need to put more money into the Social Security Trust Fund. That's part of my commitment to raise taxes on the wealthy. My Social Security payroll contribution will go up, as will Donald's, assuming he can't figure out how to get out of it. But what we want to do is to replenish the Social Security Trust Fund . . .*

At that point, Donald Trump interrupted her (as he had done so many times throughout all three debates). "Such a nasty woman," he growled.

This, from someone who just minutes earlier had said, "Nobody has more respect for women than I do. Nobody."

By uttering that phrase, Donald Trump clearly wanted to cut Hillary down to size—because, in his mind, women who speak up and take a stand are *nasty*. But girls and women across the country didn't buy it. Within minutes after Trump made that statement, the hashtag #NastyWoman started trending on Twitter. Hackers grabbed the URL www.nastywomengetshitdone.com, which automatically redirected to Hillary Clinton's official campaign website. And that night, Spotify saw a 250% play spike in Janet Jackson's hit song, "Nasty," a song inspired by a confrontation Janet had with a group of male street harassers who threatened her sexually outside a hotel in Minneapolis. Clearly, girls and women weren't going to take it.

Let's go back thirty years to 1986, when Janet Jackson's album *Control* was released. Ronald Reagan, who ushered in a new era of conservatism and anti-feminism, was serving in his second term as president of the United States. Antonin Scalia, who later wrote some of the most anti-feminist court opinions in history, was appointed to the Supreme Court. Benazir Bhutto, a Pakistani activist (and later the first female prime minister) who inspired people like Malala Yousafzai, returned to Pakistan after living in exile for eight years. And Corazon Aquino narrowly defeated dictator Ferdinand Marcos in the Philippines snap elections, although Marcos claimed the win by committing election fraud.

Wait. That last item sounds kind of familiar, doesn't it?

Corazon Aquino was a housewife in the Philippines. She hadn't been involved in politics at all, although her husband, Benigno (nicknamed "Ninoy") had, at least until Ferdinand Marcos' regime came into power. Ninoy actively resisted Marcos' oppressive dictatorship, and he was arrested and imprisoned because of his opposition. Later, he had heart trouble, and in 1980, Ninoy and his family were given permission to go to the United States so he could undergo coronary bypass surgery. They stayed in the U.S. until 1983. At that point, Ninoy wanted to return to the Philippines to try to restore his homeland to democracy. Moments after arriving and stepping off the plane, Ninoy was assassinated.

That's when Corazon Aquino became active in politics. After Ninoy's assassination, opposition towards Marcos grew, and Corazon took over leadership of the opposition party. In November 1985, an American journalist dared Marcos to run for office in a legitimate election—and he did. He declared that a "snap election" would be held in February 1986, a move that was probably a way to prove his legitimacy to the Filipino people.

One million people signed a petition encouraging Corazon to run against Marcos, and she became the UNIDO (United Opposition) candidate for president. In response to her candidacy, Marcos went on the offensive and used his campaign platform to attack Corazon in any way he could—even going so low as to say that she was "just a housewife" whose place was in the bedroom, not in politics. Election Day was characterized by massive fraud, voter intimidation, and violence, and Ferdinand Marcos declared himself the winner.

That didn't stop Corazon. After the election, she led the People Power Revolution (PPR), which demonstrated their opposition to the election results by organizing peaceful acts of civil disobedience. Opposition to Marcos' regime grew, and by the end of February, Corazon Aquino was named president of the Philippines.

After Corazon was elected president, many radical reforms took place, many of them grounded in civil liberties and human rights. Under her leadership, a new constitution was drafted to restore the country to democracy. Instead of resorting to violence, she engaged in peace talks with communist insurgents and Muslim secessionists. She also focused on strengthening the economy, and succeeded in paying off $4 billion of the country's outstanding debts. Corazon was also a member of the Council of Women World Leaders, which was an organization focused on empowering women to take on leadership roles. In 1992, Corazon decided not to seek reelection, believing that leadership should be shared among many rather than held by one. She remained active in politics throughout her life, and she died of cancer in 2009.

Many people devoted to feminism, anti-racism, and social justice were deeply disturbed by Donald Trump's election to the U.S. presidency. Corazon Aquino's story is a strong reminder of just how powerful girls and women can be, even when the opposition seems impossible to challenge. Ferdinand Marcos believed that women, particularly housewives, amount to nothing. Corazon Aquino proved otherwise.

TRY THIS!

Have you ever read something that made you cringe because it was so sexist? Or racist, or homophobic, or classist, or all of the above, wrapped up in one? When you read it, did you want to rip it up into tiny little pieces (or punch your computer screen)? Blackout poetry is a great way to create something new and beautiful out of something terrible. If you're not familiar with blackout poetry, now's your chance to learn! It operates on the principle of "less is more"—by the end of the activity, there will be very few words left on the page, but the words you chose will have enormous power.

Let's create blackout poetry! For this activity, you'll need the following materials:

- A pencil
- A black Sharpie pen
- A newspaper article, magazine article, article from the Internet, or a photocopied page from a book. Feel free to use the most horrible and offensive piece of writing you can find.

Before you read the page, look for an anchor word—a word that stands out because it has meaning for you. Circle the anchor word lightly with your pencil. Now read the page in its entirety, circling any words that connect to the anchor word. Try not to circle too many words in a row—you want them to be spread out.

On a separate piece of paper, list all of your circled words, in order that they appear on the page. The words you use for your poem need to stay in this order, so the reader won't get confused. Now, choose the words you want to use in your poem. You can use whole words, or you can use parts of words. Play with a range of possibilities before you settle on your final poem.

Go back to your text, and erase the circles around the words you won't be using. Using a black Sharpie, put a rectangle around the words you want to use in your poem. Then black out the rest of the page. Now you have a blackout poem!

If you know how to use the highlighting function on Microsoft Word, you can also create blackout poetry on your computer.

Here's an example I created. This is from an article printed in the *New York Times*, titled "Donald Trump Calls Allegations by Women 'False Smears'" (The *New York Times*, October 14, 2016).

Now create your own!

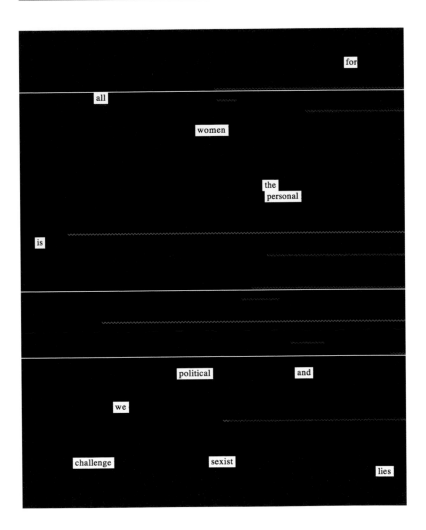

26 WAYS TO TAKE FEMINIST ACTION—TODAY!

ACT against oppression.

BOYCOTT businesses and corporations that engage in anti-feminist and otherwise oppressive practices. You can find socially responsible companies by using Green America's "responsible shopper" directory (http://www.greenamerica.org/programs/responsibleshopper/). Corporate Responsibility Magazine (http://www.thecro.com) publishes an annual list of the most socially responsible companies.

CHALLENGE gender assumptions and expectations.

DO one thing every day that scares you. (This is a famous quote by Eleanor Roosevelt.)

EDUCATE yourself and others about women's history, women's movements, and global women's issues.

FIND others who are interested in feminist issues and develop a support network.

GET angry—and then take action in an intentional way.

HANG a feminist poster in your room.

INVITE boys and men to participate in feminist actions.

JOIN a social justice organization and get involved! Here are some examples of national and international organizations. If your community has a local organization devoted to feminist principles and action, join that!

- **Black Lives Matter:** An organization that was created in the wake of the acquittal of George Zimmerman, who shot and killed a 17-year-old African-American boy named Trayvon Martin. Black Lives Matter is an effort to rebuild the Black liberation movement.
- **Equality Now:** An international human rights organization dedicated to action for the civil, political, economic, and social rights of girls and women.
- **The Feminist Majority Foundation:** An organization that believes that feminists are the majority of the population, but that majority needs to be empowered. The Feminist Majority Foundation uses research and action to empower women economically, socially, and politically.
- **Girls, Incorporated:** An organization that empowers girls to overcome obstacles in their lives and succeed.
- **GSA Network:** A queer/LGBTQ racial and gender justice organization that empowers and trains queer, trans, and allied youth leaders to advocate, organize, and mobilize an intersectional movement for safer schools and healthier communities.
- **National Coalition Against Domestic Violence (NCADV):** An organization working to end domestic violence by affecting public policy, increasing understanding of the impact of domestic violence, and providing programs and education.
- **National Organization for Men Against Sexism:** An activist organization devoted to promoting change for men through pro-feminist, gay/LGBT affirmative, anti-racist, and social justice principles.
- **National Organization for Women:** Founded in 1966, NOW is the oldest liberal feminist organization in the world, working to

achieve and protect the equal rights of all women and girls in all aspects of social, political, and economic life.

- **Planned Parenthood:** An organization dedicated to providing safe and accessible reproductive health services, sex education, and information to everyone.
- **Rape, Abuse, and Incest National Network (RAINN):** The largest anti-sexual violence organization in the United States.
- **Revolutionary Association of the Women of Afghanistan (RAWA):** The oldest political/social organization of Afghan women struggling for peace, freedom, democracy, and women's rights in Afghanistan.
- **Young Women's Freedom Center:** A leadership and advocacy organization for cis and trans young women of color that have grown up in poverty, been involved with the juvenile justice system, and experienced life on the streets.

KNOW thyself, and trust your instincts.

LOVE your body. Take good care of it. And decorate your body in a way that makes you feel good.

MONITOR your media consumption. Engage with media that's positive and empowering. Find media that mirrors your experiences, and that allows you to learn about other kinds of people. Don't consume media that makes you feel bad about yourself.

NURTURE yourself. As the feminist poet and essayist Audre Lorde once said, "Caring for myself is not self-indulgence, it is self-preservation, and that is an act of political warfare."

ORGANIZE a feminist action.

PARTICIPATE in grassroots activism. Here are some ways to get involved:

- **The Clothesline Project:** The Clothesline Project honors women survivors as well as victims of intimate violence. You can start a

Clothesline Project by encouraging girls and women who have experienced violence to come forward and design a shirt. Victims' families and friends are also invited to participate. These shirts are then hung on a public clothesline so that people can be educated about violence against women.

- **Ladyfest:** A community-based, inclusive, not-for-profit global music and arts festival for feminist and women artists. Many communities host Ladyfest events, or you can organize your own!
- **SlutWalk:** A transnational movement of protest marches calling for an end to rape culture. Participants are invited to wear whatever they want, including revealing, sexy, "slutty" attire, as an act against policing women's clothing choices.
- **Take Back the Night:** An international collection of marches where women and men take to the streets to protest violence against women.
- **Trans March:** An annual march that usually takes place during local Pride celebrations, organized by trans communities to create visibility and address human rights issues.
- **V-Day and One Billion Rising:** A series of events held every February to raise awareness about violence against women.

QUESTION everything.
READ. A lot. Here's a starter list for you:

- *We Should All Be Feminists* by Chimamanda Ngozi Adichie
- *Manifesta: Young Women, Feminism, and the Future* by Jennifer Baumgardner and Amy Richards
- *Our Bodies, Ourselves* by the Boston Women's Health Collective
- *Gender Trouble* by Judith Butler
- *Black Feminist Thought* by Patricia Hill Collins
- *Women, Race, and Class* by Angela Davis

- *The Second Sex* by Simone de Beauvoir
- *This Bridge Called My Back* by Cherríe Moraga and Gloria Anzaldúa
- *The Vagina Monologues* by Eve Ensler
- *Backlash: The Undeclared War Against American Women* by Susan Faludi
- *The Feminine Mystique* by Betty Friedan
- *Bad Feminist* by Roxane Gay
- *Feminism Is for Everybody* by bell hooks
- *Sister Outsider* by Audre Lorde
- *Whipping Girl* by Julia Serano
- *Outrageous Acts and Everyday Rebellions* by Gloria Steinem
- *Full Frontal Feminism: A Young Woman's Guide to Why Feminism Matters* by Jessica Valenti
- *The Beauty Myth* by Naomi Wolf
- *A Vindication of the Rights of Woman* by Mary Wollstonecraft

SPEAK your mind, even if your voice shakes. (This is a famous quote by Maggie Kuhn.)

TAKE a self-defense class that's grounded in ending violence against women and girls.

UNITE with people from other marginalized groups.

VOLUNTEER at a rape crisis center, domestic violence shelter, or women's health clinic. Talk to victims of rape and domestic violence. Be a volunteer escort at an abortion clinic. These experiences will change your life.

WATCH a feminist documentary. Here are several examples:

- *After Tiller* follows the four remaining doctors in the U.S. who perform third-trimester abortions.
- *The Business of Being Born* explores the world of childbirth in the U.S., inspired by Ricki Lake's disappointing hospital birth experience.

- *Dark Girls* explores the prejudices that dark-skinned girls and women face throughout the world.
- *Girl Rising* tells the stories of nine girls from around the world who overcome obstacles in order to get an education.
- *The Invisible War* investigates the issue of sexual assault in the military.
- *Killing Us Softly 4* analyzes the way in which advertising influences our attitudes about girls and women.
- *The Life and Times of Rosie the Riveter* profiles five women who entered the workforce during World War II to "do the job he left behind."
- *Made in L.A.* follows three Latina immigrant garment workers in their efforts to gain basic labor protections.
- *Miss Representation*, featuring a range of well-known media and political figures, is an exploration of sexism within the media industry.
- *She's Beautiful When She's Angry* chronicles the beginning of the women's liberation movement in the 1960s.
- *Tough Guise* addresses the link between masculinity and violence in the media.
- *Women Art Revolution* documents the rise of the women's/feminist art community.

EXPECT nothing but the best for yourself.

YELL so everyone can hear you.

ZAP sexism with all of your amazing superpowers!

BIBLIOGRAPHY

Why Teens Need Feminism

Breslau, J., et al. (2017). Sex differences in recent first-onset depression in an epidemiological sample of adolescents. *Translational Psychiatry*, 7. doi:10.1038/tp.2017.105. Retrieved from http://www.nature.com/tp/journal/v7/n5/full/tp2017105a.html#aff1.

Centers for Disease Control and Prevention. (2017). *Sexually transmitted diseases: Adolescents and adults.* Retrieved from https://www.cdc.gov/std/life-stages-populations/adolescents-youngadults.htm.

Davis, A. (2008). *Interpersonal and physical dating violence among teens.* The National Council on Crime and Delinquency. Retrieved from http://www.nccdglobal.org/sites/default/files/publication_pdf/focus-dating-violence.pdf.

Kost, K., & Maddow-Zimet, I. (2016). *U.S. teenage pregnancies, births and abortions, 2011: National trends by age, race and ethnicity.* New York, NY: Guttmacher Institute. Retrieved from https://www.guttmacher.org/report/us-teen-pregnancy-trends-2011

Mellin, L., McNutt, S., Hu, Y., Schreiber, G. B., Crawford, P., & Obarzanek, E. (1997). A longitudinal study of the dietary practices of black and white girls 9 and 10 years old at enrollment: The NHLBI growth and health study. *Journal of Adolescent Health*, 20(1), 27–37.

Partnership for Drug-Free Kids. (2013). *The partnership attitude tracking study: Teens and parents, 2013.* Retrieved from https://drugfree.org/wp-content/uploads/2014/07/PATS-2013-FULL-REPORT.pdf.

B is for Brain

American Psychological Association Presidential Task Force on Adolescent Girls. (n.d.). *A new look at adolescent girls.* Washington, DC: American Psychological Association. Retrieved from http://www.apa.org/pi/families/resources/adolescent-girls.aspx.

Pham, C., Keenan, T., & Han, B. (2013). Evaluating impacts of early adolescent romance in high school on academic outcomes. *Journal of Applied Economics and Business Research*, 3(1), 14–33.

Rosenthal, R., & Jacobsen, L. (1968). *Pygmalion in the classroom: teacher expectation and pupils' intellectual development.* New York, NY: Holt, Rinehart and Winston.

Shih, M., Ambady, N., Richeson, J. A., Fujita, K., & Gray, H. M. (2002). Stereotype performance boosts: The impact of self-relevance and the manner of stereotype activation. *Journal of Personality and Social Psychology*, 83, 638–647.

Shih, M., Pittinsky, T. L., & Ambady, N. (1999). Stereotype susceptibility: Identity salience and shifts in quantitative performance. *Psychological Science*, 10, 80–83.

C is for (non)Conformity

Asch, S. E. (1951). Effects of group pressure on the modification and distortion of judgments. In H. Guetzkow (Ed.), *Groups, leadership and men* (pp. 177–190). Pittsburgh, PA: Carnegie Press.

Darley, J. M., & Latané, B. (1968). Bystander intervention in emergencies: Diffusion of responsibility. *Journal of Personality and Social Psychology, 8,* 377–383. doi:10.1037/h0025589. Retrieved from http://psycnet.apa.org/journals/psp/8/4p1/377.

Latané, B., & Darley, J. M. (1968). Group Inhibition of Bystander Intervention in Emergencies. *Journal of Personality & Social Psychology, 10*(3), 215–221.

D is for Don't

Jones, K., Peddie, C. I., Gilrane, V., King, E. B., & Gray, A. (in press). Not so subtle: A meta-analytic investigation of the correlates of subtle and overt discrimination. *Journal of Management.*

E is for Easy-Bake Oven

Bem, S. L. (1981). Gender schema theory: A cognitive account of sex typing. *Psychological Review, 88*(4), 354–364.

Bem, S. L. (1993). *The lenses of gender: Transforming the debate on sexual inequality.* New Haven, CT: Yale University Press.

Thorne, B. (1993). *Gender play: Girls and boys in school.* New Brunswick, NJ: Rutgers University Press.

F is for Family Life

Kohler, P. K., Manhart, L. E., & Lafferty, W. E. (2008). Abstinence-only and comprehensive sex education and the initiation of sexual activity and teen pregnancy. *Journal of Adolescent Health, 42*(4), 344–351. Retrieved from https://www.ncbi.nlm.nih.gov/pubmed/18346659.

Lindberg, L. D., & Maddow-Zimet, I. (2012). Consequences of sex education on teen and young adult sexual behaviors and outcomes. *Journal of Adolescent Health, 51*(4), 332–338. Retrieved from https://www.guttmacher.org/article/2012/10/consequences-sex-education-teen-and-young-adult-sexual-behaviors-and-outcomes.

Rubin, G. (1975). The traffic in women: Notes on the 'political economy' of sex. In R. R. Reiter (Ed.), *Toward an Anthropology of Women* (pp. 157–210). New York, NY: Monthly Review Press.

Rubin, G. (1984). Thinking sex: Notes for a radical theory of the politics of sexuality. In C. Vance (Ed.), *Pleasure and Danger: Exploring Female Sexuality* (pp. 267–319). Boston, MA: Routledge & Kegan Paul.

UNFPA. (2015). *Emerging evidence, lessons and practice in comprehensive sexuality education: A global review.* Paris, France: United Nations Educational, Scientific and Cultural Organization. Retrieved from: http://www.unfpa.org/publications/emerging-evidence-lessons-and-practice-comprehensive-sexuality-education-global-review.

G is for Geek
U.S. Equal Employment Opportunity Commission. (2016, May). *Diversity in high tech.* Retrieved from https://www.eeoc.gov/eeoc/statistics/reports/hightech/upload/diversity-in-high-tech-report.pdf.

H is for Hero(ine)
Glick, P., et al. (2000). Beyond prejudice as simple antipathy: Hostile and benevolent sexism across cultures. *Journal of Personality and Social Psychology, 79*(5), 763–775. doi:10.1037//0022-3514.79.5.76
Kingston, M. H. (1976). *The woman warrior: Memories of a girlhood among ghosts.* New York, NY: Alfred A. Knopf.
Nagoshi, J. L., Adams, K. A., Terrell, H. K., Hill, E. D., Brzuzy, S., & Nagoshi, C. T. (2008). Gender differences in correlates of homophobia and transphobia. *Sex Roles, 59*(7–8), 521–531. doi: 10.1007/s11199-008-9458-7. Retrieved from https://link.springer.com/article/10.1007%2Fs11199-008-9458-7.
Robnett, R. D., & Leaper, C. (2013). "Girls don't propose! Ew." A mixed-methods examination of marriage tradition preferences and benevolent sexism in emerging adults. *Journal of Adolescent Research, 28,* 96–121.

I is for Intersectionality
Friedan, B. (1963). *The feminine mystique.* New York, NY: W. W. Norton.
Moraga, C., & Anzaldúa, G. (Eds.). (1981). *This bridge called my back: Writings by radical women of color.* Albany, NY: Kitchen Table/Women of Color Press.
The Combahee River Collective. (1986). *The Combahee River Collective Statement: Black Feminist Organizing in the Seventies and Eighties.* Albany, NY: Kitchen Table/Women of Color Press.

J is for Joke
Byrd, A., & Tharps, L. L. (2014). *Hair story: Untangling the roots of Black hair in America.* New York, NY: St. Martin's Griffin.

K is for Knitting
Baumgardner, J., & Richards, A. (2000). *Manifesta: Young women, feminism, and the future.* New York, NY: Farrar, Straus & Giroux.

L is for Literacy
de la Peña, M. (2013, November 11). Sometimes the 'tough teen' is quietly writing stories [Blog post]. *Code Switch.* National Public Radio. Retrieved from http://www.npr.org/sections/codeswitch/2013/11/11/243960103/a-reluctant-reader-turns-ya-author-for-tough-teens.
Loveless, T. (2015). *The 2015 Brown Center report on American education: How well are American students learning?* Washington, DC: The Brookings Institution.
Sommers, C. H. (2013). School has become too hostile to boys. *Time.* Retrieved from http://ideas.time.com/2013/08/19/school-has-become-too-hostile-to-boys/.

Sommers, C. H. (1994). *Who stole feminism? How women have betrayed women.* New York, NY: Simon & Schuster.

Sommers, C. H. (2000). *The war against boys: How misguided policies are harming our young men.* New York, NY: Simon & Schuster.

Wetheridge, L. (2016). *Girls' and women's literacy with a lifelong learning perspective: Issues, trends, and implications for the Sustainable Development Goals.* Paris, France: UNESCO.

M is for Media

American Psychological Association, Task Force on the Sexualization of Girls. (2007). *Report of the APA Task Force on the Sexualization of Girls.* Washington, DC: American Psychological Association. Retrieved from http://www.apa .org/pi/women/programs/girls/report-full.pdf.

Jhally, S., & Kilbourne, J. (2010). *Killing us softly 4: Advertising's image of women* [Motion picture]. Northampton, MA: Media Education Foundation.

Lazarus, M., & Wunderlich, R. (1979). *Killing us softly* [Motion picture]. Cambridge, MA: Cambridge Documentary Films.

Shoket, Ann. (2012, August). Seventeen magazine's Body Peace Treaty. *Seventeen.* New York, NY: Hearst Digital Media.

N is for No!

Freud, S. (1997). *Dora: An analysis of a case of hysteria.* New York, NY: Touchstone. (Original work published 1963)

O is for Options

Funari, V., & Query, J. (2000). *Live Nude Girls Unite!* [Motion picture]. New York, NY: First Run Features.

Gilman, C. P. (1899). *The yellow wallpaper.* Boston, MA: Small & Maynard.

Truth, S. (1851). *Ain't I a woman?* Retrieved from http://etc.usf.edu/lit2go/185/civil-rights-and-conflict-in-the-united-states-selected-speeches/3089/aint-i-a-woman/.

P is for Privilege

McIntosh, P. (1989). *White privilege and male privilege: A personal account of coming to see correspondences through work in women's studies.* Boston, MA: Wellesley College Center for Research on Women.

Q is for Queer

Queer Feminism: Radical Opposition to Patriarchy. (2016). *What is queer feminism?* Retrieved from http://queerfeminism.com/what-is-queer-feminism.

R is for Radical

Swanson, E. (2013, April 16). Poll: Few identify as feminists, but most believe in equality of sexes [Online poll]. *The Huffington Post.* Retrieved from http://www .huffingtonpost.com/2013/04/16/feminism-poll_n_3094917.html.

S is for Supergirl

Hill, C., Miller, K., Benson, K., Maatz, L., Nielson, K., Bibler, K., & VanKanegan, A. (2017). *The simple truth about the gender pay gap: Spring 2017 edition*. Washington, DC: American Association of University Women. Retrieved from http://www.aauw.org/resource/the-simple-truth-about-the-gender-pay-gap/.

Hochschild, A. R. (2012). *The second shift: Working families and the revolution at home*. New York, NY: Penguin.

Hochschild, A. R. (1983). *The managed heart: Commercialization of human feeling*. Berkeley, CA: University of California Press.

Ahrens, G. (Ed.). (2004). *Lucy Parsons: Freedom, Equality & Solidarity—Writings & Speeches, 1878–1937*. Chicago, IL: Charles H. Kerr Publishing.

T is for Tough

Douglass, F. (1888, April 14). On woman's suffrage. *Woman's Journal*.

Jhally, S., & Katz, J. (1999). *Tough guise: Violence, media, & the crisis in masculinity* [Motion picture]. Northampton, MA: Media Education Foundation.

Kalish, R., & Kimmel, M. (2010). Suicide by mass murder: Masculinity, aggrieved entitlement, and rampage school shootings. *Health Sociology Review*, *19*(4), 451–464.

Mill, J. S. (1869). *The subjection of women*. London, UK: Longmans, Green, Reader & Dyer.

Truman, J. L., & Morgan, R. E. (2016). *Criminal victimization, 2015*. Washington, DC: Bureau of Justice Statistics. Retrieved from https://www.bjs.gov/content/pub/pdf/cv15.pdf.

U is for Uterus

Koyami, E. (2003). The transfeminist manifesto. In R. Dicker & A. Piepmeier (Eds.), *Catching a wave: Reclaiming feminism for the twenty-first century*. Boston: Northeastern University Press. (Original work published 2001)

V is for Violence

Ensler, E. (2007). *The Vagina monologues*. New York: Villard.

Ensler, E. (2015, January 19). Eve Ensler: I never defined a woman as a person with a vagina. *Time*.

Kingkade, T. (2015, January 16). Mount Holyoke cancels 'Vagina Monologues' for not being inclusive enough. *The Huffington Post*. Retrieved from http://www.huffingtonpost.com/2015/01/16/vagina-monologues-mount-holyoke_n_6487302.html.

W is for Woman Trouble

58th Assembly District, California. (2016, January 5). *Assembly member Garcia Introduces "No Tax" on Feminine Hygiene Products Measure on the First day of Session* [Press release]. Retrieved from https://a58.asmdc.org/press-release/assemblymember-garcia-introduces-%E2%80%9Cno-tax%E2%80%9D-feminine-hygiene-products-measure-first-day.

Cooke, R. (2011, November 12). Gloria Steinem: 'I think we need to get much angrier.' *The Guardian.* Retrieved from https://www.theguardian.com/books/2011/nov/13/gloria-steinem-interview-feminism-abortion.

Steinem, G. (1978). If men could menstruate. *Ms. Magazine.* Arlington, VA: Liberty Media for Women.

X is for XL

Bacon, L. (2008). *Health at every size: The surprising truth about your weight.* Dallas, TX: BenBella Books.

Fishman, S., & Freespirit, J. (1973). *The fat liberation manifesto.* Los Angeles, CA: Fat Underground.

Louderback, L. (1970). *Fat power: Whatever you weigh is right.* Bristol, UK: Hawthorn Books.

Orbach, S. (1981). *Fat is a feminist issue.* New York, NY: Paddington Press.

Schoenfielder, L., & Wieser, B. (1983). *Shadow on a tightrope: Writings by women on fat oppression.* San Francisco, CA: Aunt Lute Books.

Wann, M. (1998). *Fat!So? Because you don't have to apologize for your size.* Berkeley, CA: Ten Speed Press.

Y is for Yin-Yang

Blackwell, A. B. (1875). *The sexes throughout nature.* New York, NY: G.P. Putnam's Sons.

Darwin, C. (1871). *The descent of man, and selection in relation to sex.* London, UK: John Murray, Albemarle Street.

Hrdy, S. B. (1999). *Mother Nature: Maternal instincts and how they shape the human species.* New York, NY: Pantheon.

Hyde, J. S. (2005). The gender similarities hypothesis. *American Psychologist, 60*(6), 581–592. doi: 10.1037/0003-066X.60.6.581

Z is for Zero

Jhally, S., & Kilbourne, J. (2010). *Killing us softly 4: Advertising's image of women* [Motion picture]. Northampton, MA: Media Education Foundation.

Kilbourne, J. (1999). *Deadly persuasion: Why girls and women must fight the addictive power of advertising.* New York, NY: The Free Press.

Transcript of the third debate. (2016, October 20). *The New York Times.* Retrieved from https://www.nytimes.com/2016/10/20/us/politics/third-debate-transcript.html.

INDEX